# 21st Century Sister

ALSO EDITED BY PATRICIA MIGNON HINDS

*ESSENCE: 25 Years Celebrating Black Women*

*The ESSENCE Total Makeover: Body, Beauty, Spirit*

# 21st Century Sister

## THE

## ESSENCE 5 KEYS TO SUCCESS

### Edited by Patricia Mignon Hinds
Introduction by Iyanla Vanzant

 Three Rivers Press ■ New York

Published by Three Rivers Press, New York, New York.
Member of the Crown Publishing Group.

Random House, Inc. New York, Toronto, London, Sydney, Auckland
www. randomhouse.com

THREE RIVERS PRESS is a registered trademark and the
Three Rivers Press colophon is a trademark of Random House, Inc.

Printed in the United States of America

Design by Debbie Glasserman

Library of Congress Cataloging-in-Publication Data
21st century sister : the *Essence* 5 keys to success / Patricia Hinds, editor.—1st ed.
1. Success—Psychological aspects.   2. Self-actualization (Psychology).
3. Afro-American women—Psychology.   I. Title: Twenty-first century sister.
II. Hinds, P. Mignon

BF637.S8 A14 2000
646.7'0089'96073—dc21        99-058208

ISBN 0-609-80358-1

10   9   8   7   6   5   4   3   2

EDITOR

Patricia Mignon Hinds

SPECIAL CONTRIBUTOR

Iyanla Vanzant

WRITERS

Mali Michelle Fleming

Pamela Johnson

Tara Roberts

Teresa Wiltz

# Contents

# Preface

## by Patricia Mignon Hinds

The twenty-first century opens for us so many opportunities to embrace success. We define success in this book as living with a sense of fulfillment, excitement, and passion—and living with a spiritual peace that fills you, through positive intent and actions.

We have entered a new age of economic strength that is ours to tap. We are riding in a high-tech environment that is still young. Where can we take it? We have opportunities to create our visions—and live them. We can fashion our futures as we want . . . and as we build them, we are going to need tools.

Our keys to success will offer you many opportunities to look inward—to get more in touch with who you are, what you want, and how you can accomplish your wishes and goals. They also will encourage you to reevaluate what is really important—getting to the substance of success instead of giving too much attention to superficial distractions.

Make this book your interactive guide by writing in it and keeping it nearby as a reminder of all the wonderful paths you can follow to realize your dreams—owning your own business, traveling to intriguing places around the world, and getting involved and making a difference. The information we share in this book can truly transform you. You will be inspired, exhilarated, and stimulated to discover new directions as you live your life as a truly fulfilled and empowered twenty-first-century sister!

# Introduction

## by Iyanla Vanzant

Sisters, love is the law of the new millennium. Think love. Speak love. Give love. Promote love in everything you do. And as you move into the twenty-first century, there are three important aspects of your life that you must nurture to empower yourself. The first, most important aspect is your relationship with God—an intimate, loving relationship with the God of your understanding. I don't care how much education you have, how much money you have, or how much you think you know or don't know. If you have an intimate, personal relationship with God, you will be able to weather any storm and accomplish any feat. That's really what it is about—getting back to that place of divinity within humanity. And I think women are going to lead the way for that.

The second most important thing for women in the twenty-first century is the relationship you're having with yourself—that honorable, honest, intimate, loving relationship with yourself.

But who are you? And before you can ask, "Who am I?" you must ask, "Who was I?" You need to have a clear understanding of your history—not just your story, but your history: who you were, what you did, what worked, what didn't work, what you had to offer, how you offered it, what you received, how much thanks you gave for it. What were the talents, the abilities, the skills that got you from where you were, from yesterday to today? You have to have a clear vision of that before you can ask, "Who am I?" Where are you in the story of your life—the page you're on right now? Are you moving from chapter one to chapter two? You have to know who you were in order to know who you are.

So, how do you treat yourself? How do you think about yourself? How do you handle yourself—not in spite of, but at all times? I know for me this has been a most critical aspect of my life and work: How do I love myself? How do I live this "law of love," make it the rule and not the exception? *If you break the law, then you will be broken,* so, sisters, what can you do?

One of the things I've learned is that the issue is not how you handle life. The issue is how well you handle *yourself* as you handle life. This is just so critical for us to understand. Reassure yourself, support, nurture, and honor yourself. Have a vision of how you want your life to be.

The third most important thing for women in the twenty-first century is to ask, "What is my vision? What is my mission? What do I see for myself, and for the world around me?" And, most important, "What do I intend to do about it?"

Start looking at yourself from the inside out. How can you not take everything that is available to you and do something good with it? When you know God, and trust God, you have that faith. Faith is a natural outgrowth of knowing God and trusting God. You are faith, but do you know that? And do you trust it?

The future is a treasure awaiting us, and we must use our God-given keys to unlock it. We've gotten so stuck in trying to make our own little, minuscule, minute lives work day-by-day that we don't see the blessings and the contributions that we have to make to the larger world. We must open our eyes and draw on God's strength. You must see how closely your life fits your vision of the future. If you see something you don't like or something that is not honorable of yourself, of your life, of what you know about yourself, of what you know about God, then you must ask yourself, "What is my intention?" Just what do you plan to do about it? After all, in the twenty-first century, you are not going to be able to just flounder around—you've got to move to a state of divine action. And you have to move with holy boldness. Holy boldness—to go into places and situations where you have heretofore failed to go.

Once you know who you are, then you have to say, "Well, who am I choosing to be?" Choice in the twenty-first century is going to be your divine honor and your spiritual breastplate. You have to make conscious choices, based on what your vision is, what your intention is, and what you desire to experience. It's no longer about sitting around and talking about what you're doing—what someone is doing to you, what they won't let you do, what you can't have, what you have to do for somebody else—that time is over! You've got to choose based on your vision and move toward that vision with a clear intent, based on a choice to experience a particular thing. So it's not just about who I am. It's about who I was, who I am, and who I am choosing to be—without fear.

Look in any anatomy book and I defy you to argue about what a divine and awesome creature you are. Your adrenals, and your kidneys, and your lungs, and your liver—they don't care about your being afraid. They're functioning every day without your opinion, without your likes and dislikes. You are divine! Get a grip—and move! Because if you don't move out of the fear, that's where you're going to stay.

That's what you had better get real clear—that it's not about self-value or self-worth, or self-satisfaction, but about the *self*. Self with a capital S. If you look at "self" with S meaning "soul," E meaning "excellence," L meaning "life," and F meaning "fulfillment," that's what it's about. Fulfillment of the soul, when you're excellent as you move through life.

Sisters, I think the twenty-first century is going to be about shaping your vision—ripping away all the labels, ripping away all the fluff. And do you know what? Some of us have wasted so much time up until now that the universe is going to do it for us. Move on your vision or you're not going to have an opportunity to do it anymore. When you start chasing the wrong man, you're going to break your leg. If you start eating the wrong food, then you're going to get a stomachache. When you open your mouth and start proclaiming negativity, you're going to experience that stuff. If you close your eyes to the truth, then darkness will cloud your vision.

With so much on the line in this new millennium, how do you keep your vision? The final thing that is so critical for us in the twenty-first century is ritual and ceremony. I'm not saying religion. Ritual is a prescribed way of doing something repeatedly with the intention of experiencing a specific result. Taking care of yourself has to be a ritual. Honoring our Creator has to be a ritual. How you move into your work—your life assignment, your mission—has to be a ritual. How you deal with other people has to be a ritual. How you maintain and nurture your vision has to be a ritual.

And we need ceremony—coming together, gathering to do things in a sacred way. Most people don't even know what sacredness is anymore because there is no place in this society where we teach reverence. We don't know what reverence is. We need to rediscover the sacred reverence for the things that we do.

Sisters have to get back to the ritual and ceremony: gathering, revering one another, revering time and our time together, revering our families, knowing that God will provide. God *will* provide. Because when you know God, you'll have all you need to heal and save yourself. By knowing that love is the law of the millennium, you will thrive in the twenty-first century and beyond.

21st
Century
Sister

# A Winning Attitude

Today is your opportunity to start fresh, renew, and take charge. What if we turn inward, find our best parts, and reinvent ourselves as new women—sisters fully acknowledging the past and wholeheartedly ready for the future?

What a gift it is to be blessed with an active mind and strong body as we step into an exciting new day and age. Since you were born, you've been learning about the world around you and your place in it. By now, you are probably familiar with the signals your body sends when it needs rest, nourishment, or exercise, when it is performing at its peak, or when it is in need of a little tender, loving care.

Yet if you're like most people, you're not all that certain how your mind functions. We all know that the mind is the guardian of our thoughts and ideas. But too many of us stop there. We don't make the connection between thought, word, and action. Unfortunately, we cannot grow and succeed in life without understanding the fundamental truths about the ways in which the mind works to shape our individual realities. If you are committed to personal growth, you must pay close attention to your thoughts.

We've been hearing in recent years a very similar message from the scientific community, where researchers are constantly discovering new evidence of the mind/body connection. Many studies support the idea that we largely determine our reality by what we think and what we believe. Just look around you. The proof of the power of thought is everywhere. The beauty of our families, the businesses we create, the art and music that enrich our lives, and our capacity to lend a helping hand to those in need are all the result of individual beliefs and dreams that got their start as mere ideas.

There may be obstacles in your way, and some of us will have more than our fair share. But if you believe it is possible to get ahead despite these challenges, you will succeed in this world. When you know that honesty and love are part of the natural order of things, you will experience situations that validate your trust and belief in other people. Your positive beliefs will attract positive experiences, just as the energy that you project—through your thoughts, words, and actions—forms your world and experiences. The distance you travel in life is determined by your attitude. That is why you must keep your mind focused on what you really want out of life. Hold fast to your dreams and believe that you can achieve them.

Having the kind of attitude that expects good things to happen actually helps shape your future by keeping you open, prepared, and ever ready to accept the many wonderful opportunities coming your way. These are not extraordinary, once-in-a-lifetime events like winning the lottery, but rather those more understated yet precious moments when the right situation and the right circumstances come together to make things "work." Do you want a more meaningful life? Are you seeking to make changes that will help bring you closer to your goals? The place to start is right where you are now—with yourself. Take that first step by developing a winning attitude. Your mind is a powerful force from which your actions are born. The many small and large everyday expressions of love in our lives flow naturally and spontaneously from positive beliefs.

Try an experiment.

Decide that you will be calm and loving for one day, that nothing will rattle you, and that no person or situation will upset your balance—*no matter what*. Take fifteen minutes before your day begins to still your mind and say, "I am calm and loving." And believe it. Even if being "calm and loving" is not your style, try it for one day. Whisper that mantra to yourself throughout the day. Smile often, choose your words carefully, and try not to express yourself with angry or impatient words. If something or someone upsets you, take a moment or two to breathe deeply and then let it go, keeping in mind your promise to yourself to go through this day undisturbed. At the end of the day, take stock of how the day went. Try to recall how it felt when you calmly handled a situation that ordinarily might have stressed you or caused you to panic. How do you feel now? Do you really feel more calm and loving?

Now spread that calm out over the course of a week and monitor your success. Evaluate your level of calm each day. Did you maintain calm or did you become stressed at certain points? Next, analyze the events of the day to see how well you were able to stay centered and what, if anything, threw you off course. Pinpointing the latter is the first step in eliminating those annoyances (both big and small) from your life. Here's one way to organize your one-week "calm log."

Day_____ Time_____

**Calm rating (circle one):**

very stressed          stressed          calm          very calm

**I feel this way because:**

_____

_____

_____

Remember, remaining calm in stressful situations is often an active pursuit. Don't stay passive when you're getting stressed out. Instead, take the steps you need to reclaim your calm.

# CHANGING YOUR MIND

Do you feel that your life is on track and in order? Are you happy with the way you live? Are you working toward fulfilling your dreams and goals? Are you pursuing that hobby you've always talked about or taking that class that will boost your professional skills? Is your life rich with healthy, loving relationships? Do you find ways to express your creativity, take care of yourself, and live according to your rules? If you were to rate your life on a scale of one to ten—ten being the best and one being not so hot—what would your score be?

If your number is hovering near the low end, don't look for explanations outside of yourself. Instead, look inward. What's lacking in your life is not a better job, a better relationship, or a better financial situation; it is a better attitude. All individual success begins with having a winning attitude. When you center your thoughts on discovering what's right for you and how you can achieve it, like a magnet you attract the conditions and opportunities to make it happen.

How do you bring about the changes in your mind that are necessary to cultivate a winning attitude? The first thing to do is believe it can be done. No matter what age you are, no matter how convinced you are about the fixed nature of your personality *(This is just how I am—I can't change)*, you must have faith and think like a winner. You can develop this faith in the same way you develop any skill—practice, practice, practice.

One of the best ways to begin your practice is to use a tool that has sustained you throughout your life—your breath. Several times throughout the day, pause and take a moment to breathe deeply. Let the air flow slowly in through your nose and out through your mouth. As you release your breath, feel your mind opening up to all of life's possibilities. Believe that you can change any programming or core beliefs that have kept you from maintaining a positive outlook. Believe that you have an inner light that glows and attracts all the blessings and opportunities you deserve.

## NEW GROOVES

We all have core beliefs—ideas about life and ourselves that we hold inside. We attract situations reflecting our values. Simply put, a core belief is healthy when it's empowering *(Good things always come my way because I am a good person)*. It can be unhealthy, however, if it is based on a negative view or self-perception that keeps us from fully loving ourselves *(My life is a mess)*. Positive or negative, our core beliefs run deep. We need to edit out the negatives and host only those core values that give us a positive outlook. Think of your mind as being like one of those old LP records with deeply etched grooves. To have a winning attitude, you need to make sure the grooves in your mind are etched with positive core beliefs.

Here's an exercise to help you concentrate on your positive core beliefs. Finish the sentence below by writing what you consider to be your best traits. Refer to them each morning and evening.

**I can expect blessings and opportunities in my life because I:**

_____

_____

_____

Here are some examples to remind you of traits you may have overlooked.

- I am kind and compassionate.
- I am intelligent.
- I am sensitive to the needs of others.
- I am courageous and I believe in myself.
- I am ready and willing to learn and succeed.
- I have everything I need in order to succeed.
- I have a strong, healthy body.

As you focus more and more on your many positive qualities, you'll find any negative thoughts fading fast.

Give yourself a gift—a beautiful journal. Every morning or evening, spend at least fifteen minutes writing about your deepest thoughts and feelings. Writing in your journal is like taking a refreshing shower. It cleanses your mind and frees you to approach the world feeling renewed. Journaling gives you a safe space to write about your fears and feelings, to unburden yourself, and to reflect on how you're living, loving, and learning. This is where you focus your hopes and dreams, and write the truth that's in your heart as you prepare to accomplish all the things you want.

Your journal is private, for your eyes only, so don't worry if you don't write like Toni Morrison or Maya Angelou. Each page is a great work of art because it contains your truth. Write whatever you're thinking and feeling: "My head hurts . . . So-and-so hurt my feelings . . . What am I doing with my life?" Anything. As you open your heart and write, your intuition will pour forth and inspire you. All kinds of ideas will tumble onto the pages: Ideas for new business ventures, thoughts to call or write a sisterfriend, dreams about the places you'd like to visit. Poetry. Songs. Art, crafts, images you want to create. Write about anything that is important to you. Everything that's beating in your heart. Write without censoring yourself. This helps you learn to express yourself without being critical or judgmental. Journal writing puts you in touch with your deeper self, your soul. It turns your ear to that still, small voice that you hear only when the chatter of the outside world has been silenced.

## AFFIRMING STATEMENTS

Affirmations are simple positive statements that guide our minds and hearts to basic, empowering beliefs about ourselves and our lives. Taking a few moments during the day to quietly repeat affirmations helps you maintain a peaceful and powerful loving vision of yourself.

It's easy to write your own affirmations. The words you choose should be in the present tense, active, and focused on exactly what you want to feel and experience. Say you want to gain confidence in speaking before groups of people. Your affirmation might be: "I am a creative child of God who speaks with joy, love, and authority." If you want to get some creative juices flowing when beginning a project, try saying: "All ideas exist in God. I am divinely inspired whenever I act on one of God's ideas." Speak from your heart and repeat your affirmations with conviction. You might even tape your affirmations inside your organizer, on your bedroom mirror, or on the refrigerator—anyplace you'll see them every day.

**Write some of your best affirmations below so you can refer to them often.**

- _____
- _____
- _____
- _____

## TRADING IN

Spend time doing a little mental gardening. Pull up and remove the "weeds"—those useless thoughts, beliefs, and negative emotions that flourish wildly in your mind, leaving you stressed out and unable to nourish your fertile ideas. Look for areas in your life where you can trade in stressful behaviors for peaceful solutions. To experience this state of relaxation, you have to slow down and discover the joys of stillness. Make a conscious effort to evaluate your lifestyle and decide what isn't serving you well and is worth trading in for something that will benefit you. For example, if you want to trade in impatience, you need to make some decisions. First, decide to be calm. Once you choose to remain relaxed and in control, stressful situations can't move you from a place of peace (or at least not for very long). Then remember there are some things that are simply beyond your control—and that's okay. When confronted by a challenge, tap into your well of inner peace—breathe, affirm yourself, and keep a winning attitude.

Another part of learning to "trade in" is taking the time to do things mindfully. Do you routinely rush through your meals? If so, you may need to trade in eating on the go for more leisurely mealtimes in which you practice mindful eating. Apply the same principle to other tasks that demand more patience, whether it's losing ten pounds, working toward a degree, or helping your child with her math homework.

**Use the lines below to zero in on those things in your life that you can trade in. We'll help with some examples.**

■ To become more _____, I will trade in _____
  (Example: To become more *serene*, I will trade in *negative beliefs, and instead seek out the positive side to every situation.*)

■ To enjoy more _____, I will give up _____
  (Example: To enjoy more *quality time with my family*, I will give up *overscheduling my days.*)

Grace Cornish, Ph.D., a social psychologist, is a self-esteem and relationship expert who has authored four books on empowering Black women. Here is her advice on creating a winning attitude.

VALUE YOURSELF. Don't underestimate yourself. Use positive affirmations like, "I am empowered just the way I am. I am guided and protected every day, in every way, by divine powers." When you incorporate affirmations in your daily routine, you will feel that surge of positive energy.

CONQUER BAD HABITS. Competing, copying, and comparing should not be part of your vocabulary. Celebrate your good qualities. Everyone has something they do well. Find out what you're good at and do it to the best of your ability.

KNOW WHAT YOU WANT. Whether it's a new apartment, a new job, or a new relationship, visualize your goal.

STAY FOCUSED. The winning formula for getting what you want is Focus + Effort = Manifestation. Whether your goal is losing weight, buying a new car, or getting a raise, you need to create a plan, implement it, stick to it—and be patient.

TAKE TIME TO UNPLUG. Pamper your spiritual, mental, and physical selves. Take care of yourself.

## TEN SISTER SECRETS OF SUCCESS

1. **SURROUND YOURSELF WITH POSITIVE PEOPLE.** As you make your way toward a new you attitude, make an effort to associate with positive, progressive people. Surround yourself with a circle of sisters who understand you and who value and encourage your growth and success. These are the folks who'll give you the support you need.

2. **TRY NOT TO JUDGE OTHERS.** You are here not to judge others but rather to understand and learn from them. Even those who seem very different from you or who are extremely challenging can teach you invaluable lessons to help you grow through life. Looking at others in a nonjudgmental manner will also help you develop a truly wonderful trait—compassion. As you practice compassion, it will be returned to you.

3. **LIVE YOUR LIFE WITH INTEGRITY.** Keep your word and hold others to theirs. When you back up what you say with action, you create focused intent and you will see the quality of your life change because you speak what you mean and do what you say. Others will respect you and, as a result, live up to their promises to you.

4. **DRESS FOR SUCCESS.** Looking your best is part of being the best. Dressing for success doesn't mean showing off or out. It's about looking and feeling "together" wherever you are. You can reflect an attitude of success by consciously choosing appropriate clothing to underscore your confidence, radiance, and style.

5. FEED YOUR MIND CONTINUALLY WITH POSITIVE, NOURISHING THOUGHTS. Consciously turn away from negative thoughts, statements, and beliefs. Fill your head with optimistic ideas. When discussing other people, avoid gossip and speak only of their achievements and positive traits—or express ideas that will support them on their own paths to success.

6. DON'T WASTE YOUR TIME OBSESSING OVER PERSONAL PROBLEMS. When you talk about the negatives around you, you only give them power to manifest in your life. Focus instead on the positives. Don't moan about your troubles. Instead, use that energy to find solutions, flip the script, and discuss your many blessings.

7. TREAT EVERYONE YOU MEET WITH RESPECT AND APPRECIATION. Don't get hung up on appearances; instead, see only the divinity that is at everyone's core. If you act as if everyone you meet is the most important person on this earth, they will return the sentiment and treat you honorably and with respect. Be open to the idea that anyone can be a blessing in your life.

8. REEVALUATE YOUR ACTIONS, YOUR WORDS, AND YOUR INTENTIONS. Self-development is a never-ending, ongoing process. Take responsibility for the circumstances of your life. If something is not going as well as you'd like, take the time to check out what you said, did, and thought to bring forth what you are now experiencing. The more self-reflection becomes a regular practice, the more you'll learn to consistently make better choices.

9. CHOOSE YOUR RESPONSES PURPOSEFULLY. In every situation,

think before you react. Carefully weigh the consequences of responding angrily versus responding with a "soft touch." Think about who will be affected by what you say and do. Are you willing to accept those long-term consequences? Choosing to respond always with love, understanding, and compassion will bring forth results that mirror those positive feelings.

10. BELIEVE IN YOURSELF. This is one of the easiest hints to remember but often the hardest thing to do. As you embark on the path of success and empowerment, you can expect a few bumps along the way. You may also get sidetracked or temporarily distracted by detours. That's okay. The path is not always smooth or straight, but it always teaches valuable lessons. Learn your life lessons. Always listen to the small voice inside reminding you of your innate power, goals, plans, and the ultimate good you want to do in the world.

## PLAYACTING

Can you recall a time when you were fearful of a certain situation and overcame your fear, not by trying to change the situation but by simply squaring your shoulders and facing the challenges, by pretending you were brave? That's how playacting works. When you act as if the perfect situation and conditions already exist, they soon will. For example, by seeing yourself as the strong, focused, successful woman God created you to be, you override the inhibitions that may be holding you back and *become* the person you are pretending to be.

Imagine yourself as a highly successful sister. How do you look? How do you speak? How do you interact with coworkers? What must you do to prepare yourself for that success? What kind of training do you need for your professional development? What organizations should you join to expand the contacts you'll need in your field? Hold a mental picture of the successful person you want to be, and then turn that vision into your reality one step at a time, making sure that "successful self" is always in your sight.

## GETTING TO KNOW YOU

What are your priorities? Where are you on that list? To have a fulfilling life, you must be willing to make yourself and your needs a priority. When you take care of yourself and your needs, you live in balance and everything you need for success falls into place.

When you are kind to yourself, you are kind to others. Your spirit is generous and forgiving. When your family needs your time and attention, you gladly offer it. When a sisterfriend needs your ear, you're there to listen. When you are strong and well cared for, you have more to give to others. Making yourself a priority benefits everyone around you.

Remember that when you're on a path to twenty-first-century success, all the personal growth you'll be experiencing will bring some changes into your life—and perhaps a few rocky moments, too. In times of challenge or transition, it's important to remember who you are—and those joys, accomplishments, values, and goals that bolster your confidence and keep you on track.

What kind of a person are you? What are some of your favorite things? What are you proud of, and what's important to you? Let's identify the things that define who you are so that you have a reservoir of personal power to tap when you need a little extra bolstering and encouragement before making your next move.

Begin by using the space below to write those special things that bring you joy. Is it a banana smoothie, or walking around the park listening to birds chirping? Is it getting up early in the morning for a thirty-minute run? Is it curling up with a good mystery novel? Is it spending a weekend getting away from it all with friends? If it brings a smile to your face, write it down.

**I feel immense joy when I:**

_____

_____

_____

_____

Now write down the accomplishments you are most proud of. Write as many things as you can think of, including such things as running a mini-marathon, completing a college degree, raising a child, or organizing a church program. Any activity you've done that filled your heart with wonder and satisfaction counts.

**I am so proud of:**

_____

_____

_____

_____

Next, jot down some of the things and ideals you value most. Is it a strong family life? A spiritual connection with God? Is it your sisterfriends? A close, intimate relationship with a partner who cherishes you?

**I value:**

_____     _____

_____     _____

_____     _____

_____     _____

Now begin to daydream about the goals and wishes you have yet to fulfill. Here we're talking about your dreams for today and tomorrow, such as owning your own home, adopting a child, beginning your own catering business. Let your imagination flow freely and note the things you want to accomplish.

(Review your list of new grooves from page 30 if you are afraid or apprehensive about writing out your innermost desires. You've already listed the reasons why you can have anything you want in life. Just remind yourself that you deserve success.)

**I most want to accomplish**

_____   _____

_____   _____

_____   _____

_____   _____

Spend time looking at your lists. It might help to keep a pencil in your hand as you scan, to circle the statements that jump out at you. You know that your lists comprise what you consider to be the best of your self, but see if you can narrow each list down to just one or two statements. These represent the _best_ of your best. Write them below.

- **I feel joy when** _____
- **I am so proud when** _____
- **I value** _____
- **I most want to accomplish** _____

For instance, one sister might write the following.

- I feel immense joy when I spend time indulging in simple pleasures, like watching a sunset.

- I am so proud of my education and my forward-thinking motivation.
- I value love, honesty, and my relationship with God.
- I most want to accomplish the personal and professional goals I have set out for myself: to be a caring partner, mother, and friend, and to become a financially independent businesswoman.

These exercises are simple, but you'd be surprised how they will help you stay focused on your positive self. In times of success, transition, or uncertainty, review what you've written at least twice a month. In addition, these statements will help forge the core of your personal mission statement. (P.S.: Keep these lists handy; they'll be useful later in the book!)

## YOU'RE ON A MISSION

You have probably seen other mission statements. From small-town restaurants to multinational corporations, many organizations use these clear, concise manifestos to put their best foot forward, to make their intentions known to employees and customers alike. You can use these same ideas to share the best parts of yourself with yourself, your family, friends, and new people you meet.

Writing your own personal mission statement is easy enough. Just look back at the narrowed-down list you just worked on, and put the "best of your best" together to speak to the mission you want to carry forth in life.

The sister we used as an example earlier might create a mission statement like this.

### My Mission Statement for My Soul

I am open to the beauty of the world. Through hard work and self-determination I now have a solid education, and my mission is to use this foundation for starting my own business. My mission is strengthened as I continue to learn about love, compassion, and honesty from my relationship with God. I will use these values to fortify my bonds with the people around me to become a caring partner, daughter, mother, and friend.

**Write your own mission statement.**

_____

_____

_____

_____

_____

_____

_____

_____

_____

_____

Once you have finished your mission statement, memorize it or put it in a private place and return to it for moments of insight and inspiration. Each time you read it you'll be reminded of your personal mission.

# Time Management, Self Management

There's no doubt about it—we sisters are definitely doing it for ourselves in this new era. We're racing ahead to the future and taking advantage of dynamic new opportunities, possibilities, and technologies. But with our lives seemingly on fast forward, sometimes we have barely enough time to do it all.

The one thing that hasn't been invented yet is a way to squeeze a twenty-fifth hour into every day. And all the cell telephones, e-mail, and the fastest, most sophisticated su-percomputer in the world can't help us when the kids are late for school, the work at hand should have been done yesterday, and the keys are . . . where? When our fast-paced lifestyles become a little hard to keep up with, we've got to keep balanced heads.

For sisters, the twenty-first century is all about taking care of business in the most efficient and effective way possible.

That's why one key to our success is time management. And once you realize that your time is yours to organize as you wish, time management becomes *self* management. Now, where are those keys?

## BASIC TRAINING

Whether you spend your day in a corporate office, working on a construction site, or juggling your children's activities and a part-time job, you know that when you're organized and efficient, your power is unlimited. Everything you need is in its right place, your tasks are done efficiently and on time, and you cruise through the day with less stress. Sound like a pipe dream? It's not; all you need is a system for making things happen—effectively and efficiently—throughout the day. It doesn't have to be formal, but it should be designed to make the most of your time and the space around you. A good way to do this is by arranging your work environment to match your work habits.

First, let's take a look at your workspace. What is in your space that you don't use every day? Where do these things really belong? Many times we keep things around us—on our desks, say—because we want them to remind us of things we need to do. The reality is that not only does this system not work well, it also creates piles so thick that you're often left clueless as to the whereabouts of something you need for the meeting about to start in five minutes. Some people spend, on average, an hour a day looking for papers on the top of their desks. Don't waste time playing detective. Clear off your desktop, clean out your drawers, and delete old or duplicate files from your computer. If you work in an office, set up your desk area so that you can get to your most important tools—computer, files, directory, important papers—in seconds. Keep your "in" and "out" boxes under control by throwing away unnecessary papers and turning simple jobs around quickly with a minimum of time and effort. Stay organized and the paper chase won't chase you!

For a workspace that's even more on target, consider creating a "hot project" area to allow yourself quick access to your priority projects. Everything you need, from research materials, computer printouts, and contact information to extra office supplies, should be kept in the same area, organized, and ready to go. That way you can make the most of your time simply by wheeling over and zooming in to work, without spending the ten to twenty minutes it might

## CREATING A HOME OFFICE

Technology is helping twenty-first-century sisters get down to business in more ways than ever before. With the addition of handheld computers, cell phones with Internet access, and portable fax machines, we now have the ability to do business virtually anywhere. So, if you choose to work at home or while you are on the move, these and other high-tech tools offer you state-of-the-art options for creating and maintaining a home office or a cyberoffice. But before you design the office of your dreams, let's begin with the basics.

SELECTING YOUR SPACE. Setting up your workspace can be challenging, but with the right tools and a little imagination, you can create a functional office in a separate room, large closet, or alcove. If you don't have the extra space, do not despair; you can create a flexible office out of a cabinet with shelves or your kitchen table. Look around your space and consider your options.

USING AN EXTRA ROOM, LARGE CLOSET, ALCOVE, OR SECTIONED-OFF SPACE FOR YOUR HOME OFFICE. If you have a separate space you can make into an office, the end product is limited only by your budget and your creativity. Besides the usual office equipment, you can add your own touches with framed prints and photographs, rugs, and refinished funky pieces from a second-hand furniture store or someone's basement, each reflecting your personal style. For an alcove or sectioned-off space, a folding screen, fabric stretched over a frame, or a bookcase on wheels affords you the privacy you need for work that requires your undivided attention. Different color paint is another great way to designate where your workspace begins and ends.

MAKING YOUR SPACE WORK. A key to making your office work for you is to lay it out the way you work. Select a comfortable chair for your workstation and task-specific lighting. Place your computer, printer, and telephone near each other so that you can access them easily. Check out your outlets and make sure they can handle the extra electrical load from your computer, printer, and fax machine. Use heavy-duty extension cords and power strips with multiple outlets. A power strip with a built-in circuit breaker and surge protector will prevent damage to your equipment in case of an outage.

Keep the clutter down by storing files in a cabinet, supplies in stackable storage bins or in a closet outfitted with shelves, and books on bookshelves or in bookcases.

NOW YOU SEE IT, NOW YOU DON'T! If you have space for only a collapsible or flexible office—one that can be set up when you need it and put away when you are not using it—any room will do. Multifunctional furniture that can be used as home and office furnishings saves you space and money. An armoire or home entertainment center converted into a workstation with a place for your computer and printer is ideal for this type of office A two- or three-drawer file cabinet can hold your files and the lamp next to your living room couch as well. A kitchen or dining room table can double as a desk or workstation for your laptop computer.

TOOLS OF THE TRADE The basics for your home office include a desk, chair, file cabinet, lamp, telephone, answering machine, computer, printer, modem, and fax machine/copier. If your home office is not your primary office and your workload is moderate, a combination fax machine, printer, and copier is an excellent addition. For higher-volume home offices, individual units may be best.

Your telephone keeps you connected, and with the information superhighway ever-broadening, an extra line for Internet access is a good idea. Ask your telephone company if they offer a high-speed DSL (digital subscriber line) service or your cable company if they offer cable modem service, which will greatly increase your speed when you are on-line. If you don't already have an e-mail address, contact an Internet provider and sign up. There's usually a monthly charge. It's best to shop around because various providers offer different packages and prices. In addition, you can optimize your telephone contacts by installing call waiting, conferencing, and caller ID.

normally take to get started. Keep a timeline or schedule of your responsibilities and deadlines prominently displayed so you can manage your projects well.

## Home Office Furnishings
Desk
Computer desk (optional)
Ergonomic chair

Filing cabinet

Wastebasket

Bookshelves

Telephone/fax stand

Lamp(s)

Desk accessories: pencil/pen holder, file holder, in-out tray

Bulletin board

Plastic floor mat (protects floors and rugs from desk chairs
with wheels)


## CYBEROFFICE ESSENTIALS

### Definition of Terms

**Computer** is an electronic machine that stores, retrieves, and
processes data. Purchase a reliable computer that has enough
RAM (random access memory), which determines how fast
your computer processes information. It should have sufficient memory—the more megabytes, the better. Your hard
drive, the permanent storage system for your software, should
be able to store your computer files without taxing the system. If you use your computer for graphics, video, or other
multimedia, then you will need substantially more gigabytes.

**Laptop computer,** or notebook computer, has exactly the same features as the full-size computer. These smaller versions travel well and allow you to work anywhere because they are battery operated. Some of the features include built-ins like modem, CD-ROM drive, floppy disk drive, and zip drive. When the battery runs down, just plug the computer into the nearest outlet.

**CD-ROM (Compact Disk–Read Only Memory) drive** is located on your processor. It expands your computer's ability in the areas of graphics, sound, and other multimedia programs. These programs are stored on CDs (compact disks).

**DVD (Digital Versatile Disk or Digital Video Disk)** is the next generation of optical disk storage technology. It is a larger capacity, faster CD that can hold video, audio, and computer data.

**Zip drive** is a storage unit for your computer files with removable disks that can hold over seventy times more data than regular disks.

**Monitor** is used to view data in your computer. A large monitor, seventeen inches or larger, makes viewing easier on the eyes. The space-saving flat-screen monitor is available, but it is more expensive.

**Printer** outputs the hard copy from your computer. It can print in black and white or in color. For clear, clean, and readable copy, check the dpi (dots per inch). The inkjet printer is more affordable than a laser printer, which is higher priced.

**Scanner** copies text and graphics, which can be stored and used by your computer.

**Fax (facsimile)** allows you to send information over the telephone line using a modem. Sufficient memory to store faxes and autofeed, which allows two or more pages to be fed automatically, are important features to have on your machine. Some fax machines work only with your computer, so ask questions when you purchase one. Multi-units—fax, printer, scanner, and copier—are an efficient way to get all of those functions.

**Modem** connects one computer to another via telephone lines. Either an external (a separate unit connected to your processor) or internal (inside your computer) modem is essential for access to the Internet and to receive e-mail.

**E-mail** is electronic mail sent via the Internet. You need an Internet address to receive and send these electronic communications. Sign up with an Internet provider for a monthly fee, but do some research because prices and service options vary.

**Cellular phone** is a portable and convenient way to stay in touch. These battery-operated telephones come with more features than you can shake a stick at. Do your research and find the telephone and package that best fit your needs.

## ORGANIZING YOUR TIME

A well-kept calendar goes a long way toward giving you a sense of order and balance at work. Some people like no-nonsense week-by-week calendars and some go for the comprehensive personal organizer; others dig decorative date books. Still more sisters are abandoning paper altogether to embrace electronic organizers. Helpful features of the electronic "date books" are that some sound a tone to alert you to an upcoming appointment and others, at the end of the day, automatically transfer tasks not completed on your daily to-do list to the next day. For simplicity's sake, note business and personal plans on the same calendar.

After you have a tidy workplace and an organized calendar, you can begin to develop a priority system for your daily, weekly, and monthly tasks. To keep first things just that—first—assign tasks various levels (A, B, and C) of importance. In the office, for example, preparing for an upcoming presentation would have an A-level priority, updating your calendar might be of B-level importance (when compared to that presentation), while returning unimportant e-mail messages might be B- or even C-level tasks. Here's an example of the priorities you might have, both in and out of the office.

## Office
A-level: Finalize changes and finish preparing report.
B-level: Return all calls.
C-level: Clear extra messages from voice mail system.

## Home

A-level: Take car in for tune-up.

B-level: Send thank-you notes for last week's birthday gifts.

C-level: Call for carpet-cleaning estimate.

Of course, regardless of priority, everything has to get done sooner or later. So, once you've streamlined your operation with the above time-trimming tactics, here's how to keep track of your activities (and get them done sooner). A great way to have an overview of the week's comings and goings is a master to-do list. The purpose of this list is to organize—in one place—all the tasks to be completed, projects that need work, and calls to be made, along with all the notes you once put on little yellow stickies, the backs of envelopes, and the odd piece of paper. All the numbers, meeting reminders, and other information you need to stay on track from day to day now belong here.

With each entry, write as much necessary information as you need to get the job done. If you have to schedule a car pool pickup after your daughter's soccer practice, include the names and the numbers of the people to contact so you don't have to go scrambling through the telephone book. Or if you need to drop off some clothes at a charity organization, make an appointment and write down the time you plan to go, as well as the address and number of your destination.

As new needs and plans arise, add to your list. This includes anything from an idea for an upcoming project to the dentist's appointment you've been needing to make. To keep the list manageable, try to limit it to twenty items. When you complete one of the items, cross it off. After you've finished half the items on your master list, transfer the remaining ten to a new sheet of paper and add ten new tasks.

Here's another great idea that may work well for you: Have a daily top-five to-do list that you can use to quickly spot-check the most important things to remember each day. By keeping track of everything that you need to do, your day will move forward on cruise control. Here's an example of how a daily to-do list might look.

## Top Five Things I Must Do Today

1. Confirm supervisor's travel plans.
2. Review office computer's new software.
3. Schedule doctor's appointment.
4. Pay bills.
5. Drop off clothing at women's shelter.

If you're a slow starter in the morning, or if you go into a slump after lunch, then you know your body's energy level fluctuates throughout the day. Here are some suggestions for making the most efficient use of your energy.

When is your peak-energy time of day?
☐ Morning          ☐ Afternoon          ☐ Evening
Because you're alert and on your toes, this is the best time to interact with people, whether it's making important calls or conducting business meetings. On the home front, it's also a good time to do anything physical, such as exercise or cleaning out a closet.

When is your low-energy period during the day?
☐ Morning          ☐ Afternoon          ☐ Evening
This is when it's best to focus on quiet, meditative activities such as reading, writing in your journal, yoga, or resting.

A final note. It's important to realize that there's a difference between working hard and working well. Too many people waste time and energy on unimportant tasks at the time of day when their energy level is at its highest, only to find they're tapped out when they try to finish a big job at another time of the day. That's why one important aspect of time management is knowing when and where to use your energy. If you're a morning person, work on your most meaningful projects in those early- to mid-morning hours. One of the best ways to be time efficient and productive is to get a sizable amount of work completed in the hours before your lunch break. However, if you're most productive after lunch, that's when you should focus on the tasks that count the most and do the lesser chores earlier in the day.

## WHERE DOES THE TIME GO?

You may be as close to perfect as you can be (wink, wink), but you're not a robot or some other kind of machine. Chances are there are some moments in the day when your focus strays, your concentration lags, or you simply don't make the most out of your time. By spotting these tendencies early on, you can nip them in the bud. Watch out for these time drains.

**Refusal to delegate.** If you're the type of person who tries to tackle everything single-handedly, it's time for you to

Sometimes a great asset can also be a real stumbling block. For example, the telephone can be an immense drain on one's time. Here are some tips to help you stay in control of the telephone (and not the other way around).

LEAVE A DETAILED MESSAGE. It sounds simple, but sometimes we need to be reminded to keep our voice mail/answering machine messages brief and to the point. Leave your name and number—and say your number slowly—at the end *and* at the beginning of your message (so that the recipient can retrieve that information quickly if he or she needs to replay the message), and keep what you have to say to a few concise questions or comments. Make the purpose of your call clear and your request(s) as specific as possible, including exactly what it is that you need and when you need a response. That way, what you want or need comes across quickly, clearly, and without any "filler." When your call gets returned, the caller will already have prepared responses for you and you won't need to spend time repeating yourself.

TAKE NOTES DURING BUSINESS CALLS. It's another one of those things that sounds obvious, but keeping a notepad near your telephone is a big help when it comes to remembering the exact content of your conversations. By writing down the main points of what is being discussed, you'll focus more on listening to what the person at the other end of the line is saying. That way, there will be little to no confusion later when you need to review what was discussed.

DESIGNATE A "TELETIME." If you have room in your schedule for a

little flexibility, block off a certain amount of time each day for returning calls. Don't disrupt your productive morning hours taking calls or
chasing people down via the telephone, unless it's urgent. Let your voice
mail pick up those calls and return them during your designated "teletime." Be efficient and keep the conversations brief, and you might only
need half an hour (after lunch, perhaps?) to make all your calls.

drive that superwoman into retirement. Taking on too much
and not sharing the load can make you ineffective, burn you
out, and arrest your professional development, as well as the
development of those around you.

**Saying "yes" when you really mean "no."** When someone
asks you to do something, ask for time to think about it,
whether it's an hour or overnight. If it's a project that you
want to do and you have the time to do it well, go for it. But
if you feel a tightening in your stomach, or have a sense that
it's going to take more time and energy than you have, then
decline. Say something like, "I'd really like to work on the
project, Bill, because it truly interests me. But my plate is so
full. If I took this on, I'd want to give it the attention it

deserves, and I can't do that now." Keep a list of your projects prominently displayed so you can manage them—stay abreast of what you're responsible for and when it's due.

**Refusal to let go.** Once you complete a task or a project, review your work, approve it or make minor changes, and then let it go. In many cases, fussing and fiddling with the final product only pulls you away from your original focus and raises the danger of missing the deadline.

**Being logged into www.toomuchinformation.com.** Everybody and her mama's got a Web site, and new trade publications proliferate like bunnies on Viagra. You've got to draw a line between what's useful and what's not. Manage it by developing a filter to screen out the things you don't need to pay attention to, so that you can focus on those things that really matter. If you don't have time to read an article at that moment, clip it or print it out and put it in a "To Be Read" file that travels with you for those times when you have a few minutes between appointments or are waiting for a meeting to start. Read your magazines and newspapers within a couple of days, keeping articles that you want to save and then shuttling the periodical on to a colleague or to recycling.

**Spending too much time with the mail.** Junk mail is just that, so throw it out unopened. Read the important stuff over the trash can. Transfer any important information or dates from your correspondence to your calendar and/or one of your lists, then toss the excess paper. Establish a place where you put all your bills (no, not in the trash can) so you can find them when you need to and pay them on time. With e-mail, delete those forwarded non-business-related messages before opening them (occasionally a joke or thought-for-the-day is worth the time it takes to open it, but often it's not). Print out the messages you need to keep, and add any info or dates from them to your calendar, as necessary. And remember, e-mail may not be as private as you think.

**Getting lost in a flurry of faxes.** As you do with the mail, toss the irrelevant stuff in the trash first. With those faxes that do require your attention but don't need a complicated response, consider writing your comments directly on the original and faxing it back or responding with a quick call.

**Spending too much time on the telephone.** Just because we're twenty-first-century sisters doesn't mean we don't like to gab on the telephone every once in a while. But if non-

Sheila, the executive director of a major nonprofit organization, was enjoying all the status that her position brought. But she was also putting in ten-hour days at the office and sacrificing time with her son, Robert, a high school student. Moreover, while she was steering the organization through smooth waters, she was missing doctor and dentist appointments and falling into bad health. A nervous stomach landed her in the hospital not once but twice.

Finally Sheila tried the Banyan Tree Life Management System, developed by Olubode Shawn Brown. The Banyan Tree helped put Sheila on the road to recovery. Later, she arranged for fifteen of her executive staff to experience Brown's one-day retreat as well.

Here are some tips from the Banyan Tree Life Management course.

WHO YOU ARE INFLUENCES WHAT YOU DO, WHICH DETERMINES WHAT RESULTS YOU'RE GETTING. "Most people start at the end of the equation," Brown says. They simply try to change their results without changing their actions and attitudes. This, in turn, is a direct cause of the results they get. So, in Sheila's case, feeling like Superwoman and trying to fix every crisis only led to her feeling overworked and suffering from poor health.

AWARENESS = CHOICE = CHANGE. If you aren't aware of habits that are holding you back, you'll be hard pressed to change them. Be completely honest with yourself and ask, "What actions and attitudes of mine are getting in my way?" What could you stop or begin doing to move your life forward?

SPEND TIME EACH DAY DOING SOMETHING SPIRITUAL, MENTAL, EMO-TIONAL, SOCIAL, AND PHYSICAL TO ENHANCE YOUR PERSONAL WELL-BEING. Now Sheila prays or meditates daily. For the mental element, she spends time each day planning the road ahead. For her emotional health, she enjoys time with her son. For her social needs, she reconnects with old friends. And for her physical health, she works out at least three times a week.

work-related chats have gotten out of hand, be honest with yourself and start trimming back. Besides, lots of companies monitor calls whether they tell you about it or not. Keep conversations with friends and family extremely brief, unless a serious situation arises. On business calls, stay focused. If there are several points to discuss, make a cheat sheet so that when you hang up, you have the satisfaction of knowing you covered every single issue.

**Slow going.** If you're a hunt-and-peck typist on the keyboard, consider a software program that teaches you how to pick up the pace. Check the software section at your local computer store or order from on-line book vendors. If you have more things to read than you have time, a speed-reading course may make it more manageable.

**Scheduling spaced-out meetings.** Why have one appointment at 10 A.M. and another at 2 P.M.? Think of how much "dead time" is created by traveling to and from meetings, as well as the amount of time it takes for you to settle back into a productive work rhythm afterward. Instead, try to schedule appointment clusters whenever possible. For example, after your two or three hours of productive time in the morning, you can schedule one or two quick meetings after lunch—and maybe even a working lunch. That way, you're making the most of your day.

## EYES ON THE PRIZE: POWER PLANNING

Now that time is on your side, just how can you make the most of it? What's the big secret to becoming a twenty-first-century sister? Well, the big secret is that there is no secret. The bottom line is that you've got to have a master plan.

One of the best ways to keep your show on the road and running smoothly is basic planning. Having a specific plan for a certain period of time—say, a year—is a big help when it comes to staying focused on your self-empowerment. That's because once you write something down in your own handwriting, you create an intensely personal link between yourself and your goal. And the more you look and review your plan, the more the words become part of the strength you need to make your dreams come true. The tools you'll use are simple: a notebook or three-ring binder divided into categories, with room to add notes and clippings that remind you of your plan. Think about setting goals in these categories, and write out your responses to the statements and questions below.

## Power Planning Categories
- Family
- Friends
- Community
- Career
- Education
- Money
- Play

**On the page for family, for example, you might ask yourself:**

- In terms of how well we work together, I'd give my family a _____, on a scale of one to ten.

- These are four or five things I would like to see happen in my family.

  _____

  _____

  _____

  _____

  _____

- The person I am least in touch with in my family is _____, and here is what I intend to do about it:

  _____

- My year's goal for my family is (e.g., planning a family reunion or a fiftieth anniversary party for Aunt June and Uncle Arnold):

  _____

- Here is a list of the tasks I must complete (and when I must have them done) to make this plan successful. (Plan backward—begin with the event itself and work back to the present.)

  _____

  _____

  _____

  _____

Next, set an objective from one of the power planning categories listed on page 71. For instance, you might decide that you want to make a difference in the lives of children in your community, or enhance your own personal development by going back to school. Write your objective here.

**I want to** _____

_____

Now come up with tasks to ensure that you fulfill that objective. To help neighborhood children, look into tutoring, mentoring, or initiating a fund-raiser to buy uniforms for the local soccer team. For your education plans, you would research various courses of study and schools (whether they be technical schools, college or universities, or adult continuing education programs) and their financing options.

**List the tasks needed to achieve each objective here.**

_____

_____

_____

_____

Use this system to establish objectives and tasks for the other power planning categories on page 71. Share your goals with other people; they may be able to help you or know someone who can. Sharing also opens natural opportunities for collaboration. To keep your ideas fresh in your mind, read through your notebook once a month, adding and pruning, and revise it each year around your birthday.

## ON THE HOME FRONT

If it's important to keep our professional lives organized, it's absolutely essential that our home lives are also well-managed. Regardless of what's going on, we need to keep our homes running smoothly in order to preserve the winning attitudes we need for success. Here are a few ideas on how to keep your house a productive home.

**Establish a routine.** Mornings go smoothly when you get a jump on them the night before. Nighttime is the right time for listening to the next day's weather report and laying out everyone's clothes—including your own. Plan simple fruit-and-cereal breakfasts. If you have children, put all the break-fast foods on one shelf in the refrigerator so the children—if they're old enough—can make it themselves. Place every-thing, including keys, that you need for the day near the front door. Also, make sure your purse/briefcase is stocked with everything you'll need.

**Keep the day on track.** If a bunch of things need to hap-pen before work or school, make a list of them and tape it to the back of the front door. Cross off each item after it's done. Keep track of all household commitments and appointments on a calendar posted on the refrigerator or in another con-venient spot. Pack the car with items you know you'll need—a tennis racket and balls for your weekly lesson, sneakers for a lunchtime walk, and change and tokens for the tolls. You might even want to consider keeping a microcassette re-corder with you to capture any to-do items you may think of without having to write them down.

**Multitask.** Double up on chores when possible. Wash and dry clothes as you dust and vacuum. Run the dishwasher as you clean out the refrigerator. Block off some time and run all your errands at once rather than squeeze them in here and there. Which activities can you pair up to get things done quickly?

**Share the load.** If you're a family of two or more, figure out ways in which your partner and/or the kids can help. Maybe while you're cooking someone can mow the lawn, or vice versa. Post a list of household chores, indicating when and by whom they are to be performed.

**Bring on the night.** If you have evening plans, choose an outfit for work that lets you make the transition, or take a no-iron shimmer top, earrings, shoes, and matching evening bag to the office with you. (You could even keep these in your office for those occasions that simply spring up.) At night, get undressed right at the closet and hang up clothes as you take them off. Keep a used clothing bin in the closet so you can put giveaways in it immediately instead of rehanging them. Rather than changing clothes to do a task, put on a chef's apron.

■ "To save time, store each bill with its statement and the due date clearly showing, file them in order, then keep them in a folder or some other place near your checkbook. When you know where everything is, you won't have to dig all the time—and that's a big stress reducer." **—Laura Savino, Task Management Solutions, Amityville, New York**

■ "Your home should be your sanctuary, a place where you go to get reenergized. Every couple of months I go through every drawer and cabinet and evaluate everything. After I get rid of the things I don't need, I feel renewed and open to abundance. The point of organization is to create order and to make life run smoother; otherwise, there's no point to it." **—Shelli Alexander, Order by Design, Los Angeles, California**

■ "You need your personal time. Even if it's only half an hour a day, be firm about taking it. You might want to work on a hobby, spend time soaking in a bubble bath with a glass of iced tea, or do nothing at all. Personal time is so vital to us because it refreshes us and prepares us to take on the other components of our lives." **—Roberta Roesch, author of *The Working Woman's Guide to Managing Time***

■ "When battling procrastination, you've got to psyche yourself up. Stop saying, 'I don't want to do this,' and replace the negative thoughts with positive ones, such as, 'This is going to come off really well, and then I can take a vacation or put in for a promotion.' When you triumph over procrastination, you feel in control. You think, 'I got it done. I powered myself through this!'" **—M. Susan Roberts, Ph.D., author of *Living Without Procrastination: How to Stop Postponing Your Life***

**Bank at home.** Many banks allow you to conduct an array of transactions, including paying your monthly bills, via your home computer. Check with your local bank to see if they offer such a service. If not, you can use a computer software program that pays your bills automatically (or when you tell it to). Look for the software in computer stores or on-line.

## OUT WITH THE OLD, IN WITH THE NEW

Clearing clutter is not only vital for time management, it can clear trapped energy, lift you out of the blahs, and spur you on to abundance. Some of us have a lot of emotions packed up in old boxes and closets, and once we get the courage to clear them out, we find that other parts of our lives get in motion as well. Here's how to S.T.A.R.T. a job and make way for smooth sailing.

**Strategize it.** Get an overview of what you're trying to accomplish; it's one of the most important and overlooked phases of a clean-up project. Set a plan of action and schedule when you're going to get to the different phases. For instance, this Saturday do that closet, and next Saturday tackle the refrigerator. Or set aside a certain number of hours to whisk through a chore. Get the job done with your own style, working with yourself rather than against yourself, and you'll be happier in the process.

**Trash it.** Let's say you're about to clean out a closet. Set up your criteria for doing the job. One way to approach it is to use boxes for various categories. You might have a box for charity/giveaways, a box for things that need to go to a different room, a box for things that need to be filed. This is a presorting process. Don't, however, sort anything if you're going to throw it away later. If you're dealing with magazines or mail, for instance, you may decide to get rid of anything that's more than six months old. If you haven't worn a piece of clothing in six months or a year, or you never liked it anyway, or you are holding on to something you hope will fit again after you lose twenty pounds, give it away. (You can always make a case for holding on to something, but be honest with yourself.) There are women's shelters that would be happy to have these garments—particularly suits, so that the women can wear them for job interviews as they get their lives back on track. Your donation helps others, makes you feel good, and can earn you a tax deduction.

**Arrange it.** Create a system for any process you do over and over again. For instance, you can start a shopping routine by taking an inventory of the household items you typically buy. Type it up on a computer or write it out neatly, have it laminated, put a magnet on it, and attach it to the refrigerator. Then you can use a red, erasable marker to indicate on it those things you need to pick up at the store. Or you could print out ten copies of your staples list, marking one up each time you go to the store. Toss it when the deed is done.

Always store similar things together. If you have a lot of books, create your own library. Take everything off the shelves and create categories. Maybe all your Black literature books will be on one shelf, and all your self-help books on another. Maybe your novels on two more shelves, and so on, until you can walk straight to your shelves and put your hands on the exact volume you want—when you want it.

**Renew it.** After you've cleaned out the clutter and created systems for those tasks you do all the time, make your space your own. In every room ask yourself, "What would make me feel good in here?" Whether it's a brilliant new comforter in your bedroom, a collection of pictures of family and friends, or a piece of sculpture for the living room, make sure your home speaks to your personal style.

**Test it.** How well does your new system work? Once you're up and running, don't be afraid to improvise a little here and there in the interest of keeping things efficient. And since you've cleared away all the excess "stuff" around you, fine-tuning is easier than ever!

## IT'S YOUR TIME

You're on your way to being a highly organized master planner. What are you going to do with all the extra time on your hands? Why not do exactly what you want? Here's how to make the most of the time you're saving.

Take a blank sheet of paper and make a column for the seven days of the week. Now pencil in your ideal schedule, answering these questions to help you along.

- What would you do if you could spend your time as you wish each day?

  _____

- What time would you wake up in the morning?

  _____

- Who would you spend your time with?

  _____

- What would you do for exercise?

  _____

- What would you do to satisfy your urge for creativity?

  _____

- What is your ideal work?

  _____

Now compare these responses to your actual weekly schedule, using the last two weeks as a reference. Slowly phase out things from the real schedule that don't empower or fulfill you, replacing them with the better things you envision for yourself. While you can't immediately swap one for the other, over time you will find that when you put your heart and mind to it, you can turn the ideal into the real.

You have all the skills you need to manage your time, your self, your life—all that's left to do is roll up your sleeves and get the job done.

GO FOR IT!

# Career Planning

From Wall Street to Main Street, we are taking care of business! We have opportunities today that Black women in the past could only wish for, and those wishes have become the careers taking us into the classrooms, courtrooms, and boardrooms of America (of course, many sisters work outdoors, too!). And once we're in those arenas, we're changing the face of our country's workplace.

Some sisters remember very clearly what, as a child, they wanted to be when they grew up. For others, deciding on a career was something that eluded them as teenagers and on into adulthood. Some of us are all grown up and we still don't know what we want to do or be. What about you? Do you have a career that you enjoy? Is there a "dream job" that you're working toward? Could you be getting more enjoyment from the career you have right now?

If you're fully content with your current career, congratulations! If you're like most of us, though, you're hungry for something a little sweeter than what you have right now—that's even better. That means the best is yet to come. And once you direct your thoughts and actions toward advancing your career or getting more satisfaction out of your work life, there'll be no stopping you.

What's needed is a career strategy tailor-made for you. When you think about the many years you spend working, the time it takes to thoughtfully evaluate your career development plans is definitely a worthwhile and cost-effective investment. Creating an action plan is a big part of getting the ball rolling toward finding a job that satisfies your needs, desires, and goals. By being honest with yourself, being prepared, doing your homework, and getting your foot in the door, you'll be on the road to fulfillment.

Don't wait. Be honest about assessing where your career is right now, so you will know what needs to be done. Don't be afraid to do whatever it takes. Be proactive and take control of developing your career. Move out of the passenger seat and into the driver's seat and go where you want, at your own speed, along a satisfying and successful career road.

# TAKING STOCK

Let's face it, many times the job or career you have isn't necessarily the one you chose for yourself. Early on, your family, friends, teachers, even your partner may have urged you to follow a certain path. Surely they meant well, but after a time you may be feeling as though you are working to meet others' expectations and not your own. It's never too late to get another plan, and the first and most important step you can take is identifying what's best for you.

The search for a satisfying career becomes much easier when you know yourself well. Take the time to conduct a personal inventory of the things you like to do, what gives you satisfaction, your strengths and weaknesses, and, of course, your goals. Grant yourself the room to really explore the many facets of your personality and style.

Do you like to work alone or with others? Do you like to travel or stay in the office? Are you an idea person or do you prefer the details? Think about what motivates you. Do you get satisfaction from helping others? Do you like to deal with numbers, keep financial records? Do you like to organize systems, people, or events?

If you need a little help figuring out what you want to do, consider career counseling. There are experts who will provide a comprehensive assessment to help move you to the next stage of your work life. They will assist you in identifying your strengths, work values, and the type of environment in which you want to work, along with the kinds of activities you prefer and the kind of questions that often come up in job interviews. By describing what you want your work life to feel and be like, you can work with the counselor to come up with a job description and a plan to get such a position.

Whether or not you seek professional career counseling, the point is to be as open and honest as possible about your ideal work life so that you make the right moves early. It's okay to dream, but be sure you figure out exactly what kind of career would suit you best. This will surely help you avoid pitfalls on your career path later on.

Take a moment to consider what kinds of work you always wanted to pursue but instead ended up putting on the back burner. Use the space below to make a list of three jobs you would love to have. Then write out your experience, skills, and the values you look for in a workplace. Once you've identified what you'd like to be doing, refer back to these lists as you develop your career plans in this chapter.

**The three jobs I want are:**

- _____
- _____
- _____

**My past experiences (jobs, internships, and volunteer work) include:**

- _____
- _____
- _____
- _____

**My skills (from computer programming to child care) are:**

- _____
- _____
- _____
- _____

**Values I look for in a workplace (from open communication to training opportunities) include:**

- _____
- _____
- _____
- _____

# YOUR MASTER PLAN

Taking time to plan your career is essential because no one is going to advance your career for you but you. And as with any journey, you need a road map to keep you on your career path.

So what's your master plan? These steps will help you craft one for your career.

## Research

To get in touch with an industry's pulse, read trade publications and search out magazine articles on your field of interest. Subscribe to them and attend local, regional, and national conventions and seminars related to your prospective path. *The Occupational Outlook Handbook* from the U.S. Bureau of Labor Statistics is an excellent resource that details job prospects in a variety of occupations, along with educational/training requirements.

Log on to the Internet, using keywords like "career" to find helpful Web sites (you can also check the resource list in the back of this book for good sites), and visit career fairs to meet and greet potential employers. You can also go to your local library's job information center to research a particular field and study those companies (both for profit and non-profit) that you're interested in. There you will find contact information on trade and professional organizations like the National Society of Black Engineers or the National Association of Black Journalists. Through these types of groups you will find recruitment opportunities, meet major players in the industry, and get reading material that puts you in touch with the issues and the future of the industry. You'll surely have an opportunity to speak directly with a member to find out more about the profession. You'll want to ask questions like: What is your job like? What do you do on a daily basis? What types of skills would I need in this field? What can I do to get into this field? Does your organization offer internships or summer jobs?

## Education/Skills

After you've conducted research on your field of interest, assess your education and your skills. Do most people in your ideal job have technical training, a bachelor's degree, a master's degree, a Ph.D.? Do you need new skills or extra training to beef up your credentials? Find out if your skills are commensurate with others in the field by consulting the

*Dictionary of Occupational Titles*, published by the U.S. Department of Labor. If you find your skills are lacking, you will need to do a little prep work. There are often opportunities to work on a volunteer, part-time, or freelance basis. Internships and summer jobs are also great ways to gain valuable experience and learn about your area of interest. With on-the-job training, you make great contacts and get firsthand knowledge of the field and a chance to upgrade your skills. These experiences will help you shape your résumé toward the career path you desire.

## Setting Goals

Goals keep you focused by stating precisely what it is you're after. If you frequently revisit the goals you've set for yourself, your thoughts, intention, and actions will fly to those plans like an arrow.

Goal setting is a three-pronged process. Create goals that are attainable in the short term, midterm, and long term. Short-term goals are those that can be achieved soon (within a year's time); midterm goals are those that can be reached in the next five years; and long-term plans focus on ten years and beyond. Here are examples of one sister's goals.

## Short-Term Goals

- I want to position myself for a promotion this year.
- I want to become an active member in a national organization for Black women.
- I want to take a business course at the local community college.
- I want to learn how to use the Internet.

## Midterm Goals

- I want to go back to college and finish my bachelor's degree.
- I want to earn a master's degree.
- I want to achieve a leadership position in a women's organization.
- I want to start a consulting business.

## Long-Term Goals

- I want to open my own fast-food franchise.
- I want to study toward a Ph.D.
- I want to save enough money to send my children to college.
- I want to build my 401(k) to retire comfortably.

Use the spaces below to write down some of your own goals.

**My short-term goals are:**

- _____
- _____
- _____

**My midterm goals are:**

- _____
- _____
- _____

**My long-term goals are:**

- _____
- _____
- _____

## GET THAT JOB!

So you've assessed your skills, education, and experience.
You've set some goals. You're ready to unleash your twenty-
first-century sister self on the working world, and when you

step out there, you want to get that job. Even when unemployment rates are low, there are lots of highly educated and skilled people in the workplace. So you must be prepared and on point to get the spot you want. Here are the basics to help you jump-start your job hunt.

### Résumé and Cover Letter

Your résumé is a snapshot of your work experience. Generally it should be no longer than one page and succinctly list your skills, education, and relevant job experience. See it as a marketing tool to help you get inside a company for an interview. Your résumé should use action verbs (see "Power Words," page 102) to describe the nature of your skills and work experience most effectively. It absolutely must be free of grammatical and spelling errors and presented on neutral, white, or light gray paper. Quality paper will distinguish you and make a good first impression.

Résumés can be organized in any of three ways: reverse chronological, functional, or a combination of both. The reverse chronological résumé lists in order each of your jobs beginning with the most recent; the functional emphasizes skills over the last position held; and the combo mixes the chronological and functional. You can decide which

## Chronological Résumé

The chronological résumé describes work history, beginning with your most recent position and working backward.

**Akira Thompson**
**895 Hunter's Way**
**Brooklyn, NY 11238**
**718-555-5555**
**athomp@linkus.com**

EDUCATION        SPELMAN COLLEGE                          ATLANTA, GA
                 Bachelor of Arts, Marketing, 1993
                 YALE UNIVERSITY                          NEW HAVEN, CT
                 Marketing Seminar
                 Summer 1992

OBJECTIVE

To utilize my skills and experience in the retail industry and attain a position as a buyer for a large retail chain.

EXPERIENCE

Rudolph's Department Store                               New York, NY

Assistant Buyer

1996–Present

Organize day-to-day office procedures essential to the promotion of sales, advertising, and buying within departments.

• Monitor purchase order process from initiation to finalization
• Develop working relationship with manufacturers to ensure timely receipt of merchandise
• Analyze profitability of styles in order to correlate markdowns within a budgeted plan
• Execute store merchandising program

Juliette's Basement                                    White Plains, NY
Manager
1994–1996
Managed children's clothing department of national discount chain store.

• Interviewed, screened, and hired candidates
• Purchased wholesale merchandise and determined markup of goods based on selling trends
• Managed accounts payables to vendors

My Mother's Closet                                     Atlanta, GA
Sales Associate
1992–1993
Assisted in the sales and operation of an upscale women's clothing boutique.

• Shopped the market for specialized merchandise including clothing and accessories
• Provided one-on-one consultation for preferred customers

AFFILIATIONS
Alpha Kappa Alpha Sorority, Member
National Urban League, Member

---

format is best for you as well as examine sample chronological and functional résumés that are presented in this chapter (see pages 96 and 98). While you're working on your résumé, think of at least three people who have knowledge of your work habits and experience and can be used as references should a prospective employer request them. Contact them

## Functional Résumé

The functional résumé highlights your skills rather than the place and time you worked. It does not focus on employers, job titles, and dates.

**Cynthia Jeffrey**
**254 Robin Crest Drive**
**Los Angeles, California 90221**
**213-555-9088**
**jbenson@aol.com**

CAREER SUMMARY
• Master of Science and Bachelor degrees in health sciences
• Eight years of individual and group health and nutrition counseling
• Extensive knowledge of wellness and preventive medicine techniques, including homeopathy, massage therapy, yoga, and meditation

EXPERIENCE
Health Promotion Specialist              Randolph Institute, Los Angeles, CA
1997–Present
• Provide nutrition testing and counseling to groups and individuals
• Conduct health and fitness classes

Health Instructor              Prairie Community College, Phoenix, AZ
1993–1997
• Taught health course to freshman, with emphasis on sex education, wellness, and nutrition
• Produced a bimonthly newsletter for student body on health and wellness information and resources

Fitness Trainer              Atlas Total Fitness, Phoenix, AZ
1991–1993
• Designed personal fitness programs for individual clients
• Taught aerobic and kickboxing exercises to developmentally disabled classes

EDUCATION
Master of Health Sciences, University of California at Los Angeles, 1990
Bachelor of Science, Occupational Therapy, University of Colorado, 1988

CERTIFICATIONS
American College of Sports Medicine, Health and Fitness Instructor, 1993
Wellspring Wellness Institute, Homeopathy and Massage Therapy, 1992

---

and ask their permission to use their names as references.

The cover letter is an introduction to your work experience and the skills outlined in your résumé. It also lets a prospective employer know how you found out about the position available and why you are the best person for it. You should use a cover letter when applying for or inquiring about a position. Keep the letter conversational in tone, yet strictly business in content. The letter should be addressed to the specific person you wish to contact, using her name and title. Be sure to get to the point immediately because most employers get hundreds (and sometimes thousands) of résumés over the course of a year. You want to capture the person's interest as quickly as possible and impress him so that your cover letter and résumé don't go into the "To Be Filed" folder, or worse, the trash. A final check: Have someone who is an expert at grammar and résumé preparation review yours before

## Cover Letter 1

**Lisa Langley**
**7332 North Rector Street, #2**
**Baltimore, MD 20414**
**301-555-0745**

July 25, 1999

Ms. Rebecca Smith
Managing Director
*The Baltimore Morning Edition*
367 Channel Avenue
Baltimore, MD 20411

Dear Ms. Smith:

I am writing to apply for the production manager position at *The Baltimore Morning Edition.* I recently met Jack Saunders at a job fair in Richmond, Virginia, and he informed me that you are looking for a production manager to handle the weekend edition.

For the past five years, I have worked as a production manager at *Good Morning Richmond.* I have coordinated production schedules and helped create story lines for the program. It has been number one in the morning ratings in the Southeast market for the last three years. In addition, I have a master's degree in communications from Howard University.

I would like to apply my skills as the production manager at *The Baltimore Morning Edition.* Thank you for your consideration, and I look forward to hearing from you soon.

Sincerely,

Lisa Langley

Encl.

## Cover Letter 2

**Debra Howard**
**9915 North Capitol Street, N.W.**
**Washington, D.C. 20011**
**202-555-3354**

April 1, 1999

Ms. Anita Banks
Director
The Bank School
21 South Capitol Street, N.W.
Washington, D.C. 20020

Dear Ms. Banks:

I am writing to inquire about a position as a special education teacher at the Bank School. I learned about your school through an article in *The Washington Post*. I was moved by the way the parents of the students talked about your curriculum and the success their children—many of whom come from lower-income backgrounds—were experiencing.

I am a recent graduate of the University of the District of Columbia and have a bachelor's degree in education. I majored in special education and I am interested in pursuing job opportunities at your school.

I am enclosing my résumé for your consideration. I will call your office in a week to schedule a time when we can meet.

Thank you, in advance, for your consideration.

Sincerely,

Debra Howard

Encl.

Below is a list of strong, active power words you can use to express yourself well and make a strong impression with your résumé and cover letter.

| | | |
|---|---|---|
| accounting | entertaining | planning |
| acting | evaluating | problem-solving |
| administering | facilitating | promoting |
| advising | fund-raising | questioning |
| analyzing | inspecting | record keeping |
| arranging | interpreting | repairing |
| budgeting | interviewing | reporting |
| coaching | investigating | researching |
| communicating | judging | reviewing |
| counseling | listening | selling |
| creating | managing | speaking |
| customer service | mediating | supervising |
| delegating | monitoring | teaching |
| designing | motivating | training |
| dispensing | negotiating | translating |
| editing | organizing | writing |

making copies. Many talented people lose out on job opportunities because of sloppy mistakes like typos, misspellings, or getting the addressee's name or title wrong. Little things like that can open or shut the door to the job you want.

## Job Hunt

The obvious place to look for work is in the "Help Wanted" section of the newspaper, but remember, the rest of the world is also looking there each day, and especially on Sundays, so you'll want to be more resourceful and creative in your search. If you identify a company that holds the values that are important to you and that you'd like to work for, then go directly to the organization and apply for a position. If nothing of interest is immediately available, stay in touch with the director of human resources, as well as with the head(s) of department(s) where you would like to work. Follow up periodically with little notes and a call. With an impressive résumé, you will be remembered when an opportunity is available.

The Internet can be another powerful tool in your job search. If you don't have Internet access at home, find a friend to help you or go to the public library and get on-line.

## Networking

Let your friends, acquaintances, and former and trusted coworkers know that you're looking for work and exactly what you want to do. They may know of an opening that would be perfect for you, or know someone else who might be able to help you in your search. Once you contact some-

## ACING A GREAT INTERVIEW

When Ruth Clark, president and owner of CUP Temporaries, Inc., started her New York City–based company in 1974, she became the first Black woman to own and operate what has become one of the largest temporary placement services on the East Coast.

Ms. Clark, a human resources specialist, shared her tips for preparing for a successful interview.

YOUR RÉSUMÉ IS YOUR CALLING CARD. A one-pager detailing your employment history, educational achievements, and professional affiliations without grammatical, typographical, or spelling errors goes a long way. Get help from a professional résumé company if you need to. Clear and concise job descriptions emphasizing your skills and accomplishments provide a short history of your experiences.

YOU ARE WHAT YOU WEAR. Neatness counts. Your appearance telegraphs volumes about your personal self. Accessorize simply so the focus will be on what you say and not on how you look.

PREPARE THOROUGHLY FOR YOUR INTERVIEW. Be on time and greet the interviewer with a warm smile and a firm handshake. Know the company and be able to ask intelligent questions. Never discuss salary in the first interview. And never bad-mouth your previous employer, it's not good form.

FOLLOW UP WITH A NOTE AFTER THE INTERVIEW. Thank the interviewer for the opportunity to discuss the position. This act of courtesy will remind the interviewer of who you are. If you haven't heard back from the company after a week, it's all right to call. Don't harass the interviewer with countless calls—be patient; sometimes it takes a while for the company to make a decision.

BE AN INTELLIGENT NEGOTIATOR. Know the going rate for the position by talking to folks in the field. Be confident and begin the dialogue. If you go through an agency or a search firm, they will negotiate your salary in collaboration with you, of course. Remember that these companies charge a fee for their services. Health insurance, vacation, annuity programs, and educational incentives are part of the benefits package. Be sure to ask questions about these perks.

TRY A TEMPORARY POSITION. It's a great way to check out a company. Tons of agencies specialize in everything from accounting, to nursing, to catering staff, to administrative support. A temp experience gives you a chance to get to know the company and vice versa; it's like an audition and many times it can turn into a permanent placement.

one in a company or business you're interested in, ask the person to show you internal job listings. This way, you'll have a leg up when applying there. Also, have business cards professionally printed and carry them with you at all times. You need to be able to hand someone your card easily, and not have to scribble your number on a piece of paper that is bound to get lost.

Join professional organizations and keep in touch with alumni from your college or university, or your sorority sisters. Meet movers and shakers in your city who belong to these organizations, especially the ones people in your chosen profession support. Often they'll know about employment opportunities not listed in the local newspaper, the ones you learn about strictly by word of mouth. As you exchange and collect business cards and make calls, keep clear records of your contacts by saving the names and numbers in a file, on your computer, or in your electronic organizer. Get a notebook dedicated to networking and write down where and when you met each person, and reasons for each contact. Any time a contact shares information, be sure to send a thank-you note (including a business card or two). Keeping in touch with contacts will help you throughout your career.

## Interview

This is the moment to share yourself and your skills. The most important thing is to stay calm, cool, and collected. Be prepared. Read everything you can about the organization. The company's annual report, Web site, and employees can give you an overview of the organization and its culture.

Get a good night's sleep before your interview. Be sure to

arrive early for the interview and dress appropriately. Even if the position you want is not in corporate America, it still makes sense to be a bit understated. A simple, smart conservative suit, short, natural-colored nails, little jewelry and makeup, and a simple, neat hair style are always appropriate. Give your interviewer a firm handshake (but don't go overboard), and always look her directly in the eye with an easy, friendly smile when speaking. Remember that the interview is an active conversation. Let the interviewer know that you are really interested in the business and have done your homework by asking questions and making informed comments on the company's performance and on industry trends.

Here are a few questions you can ask.

- When do you expect to fill the position?
- What types of skills are you looking for with this position?
- What are the responsibilities of this position?

Here are a few questions that may be asked of you.

- What are your short-term and long-term goals?
- What are your strengths and weaknesses?
- Where do you see yourself in the next five years?

## DRESS FOR SUCCESS

While obviously your focus in the office should be on the quality of your work, it never hurts—and sometimes helps a great deal—to have a well-put-together wardrobe for work. It has long been a strategy of successful people to dress for the position they aspire to. Mixing professional attire with a dash of personal style is one way to say "I know the rules and how to maintain my individuality at the same time." Know your body type and the lines and proportions that suit you best. Stay within that arena and look for exquisitely made clothes in fine, durable fabrics.

MAKE A GOOD IMPRESSION. Play it safe in the beginning by checking out what your coworkers and superiors are wearing; that way you'll have a good idea of the standard of what's considered acceptable dress in your office.

DEVELOP METICULOUS STYLE. Hold a standard for yourself that ensures that your hair, nails, and clothing are always neat, clean, and meticulously put together, and make sure your work standards are the same. P.S.: Never overlook fresh breath.

PLAN WHAT YOU'LL WEAR EVERY DAY. Lay out what you'll wear the evening before. Not only will this save time on busy mornings, but deciding what to wear ahead of time gives you a better opportunity to see what works as an ensemble—and what doesn't.

DRESS CONSERVATIVELY. Neutral colors and classic cuts (low hemlines and little cleavage) are best. You can easily build on these basics each season. Keep jewelry to a minimum; remember, you want people to focus on you, not your accessories.

# MAKE YOUR MARK

As with any new relationship, it's important to start a new job on the right foot. Here's how to set yourself apart from the pack.

- Every day, come in the door focusing on what you were hired to do.
- Develop a relationship with people in your field who are successful and have a passion for what they are doing.
- Establish who you are—your work ethic and professional style—as soon as you start your new position. Make your mark and be known as a competent, consistent team player. Always be on time for work and meetings.
- Focus on understanding and developing your own special skills; it will set you apart as an individual with a lot to contribute.
- Ask well-thought-out questions. It puts people on notice that you are aware, alert, and an active participant in the organization.
- Information is power. Understanding the full extent of your responsibilities (and the benefits they bring) is part of developing your niche in the workplace.

- Maintaining a list of your projects is a good way to keep track of your accomplishments inside the company.
- When you develop a good track record, people will ask to work with you. Developing a reputation for getting the job done will bring opportunities that come about based on knowledge of you and your work alone.
- Join organizations that focus on the social well-being of your community, such as the Urban League and NAACP. These types of organizations offer great networking, as well as mentoring and educational opportunities, and industry-specific information about who's hiring.

The good work you do to help our people move forward and to become active in your industry's professional organization plays a major role in your success. Here are a few tips on establishing yourself and your value in your career.

**Have a positive attitude.** Wear a smile and know that you are an asset to your organization. Plan to succeed. Have faith in yourself and know that you can accomplish any task. You may not be able to do everything yourself, though, so don't ever be afraid to ask for help.

**Keep up with technology.** Technological advances happen so quickly these days, it's absolutely essential that you keep track of the basics. You don't have to be a "techie," but you should have a working knowledge of the Internet and e-mail, and some understanding of or experience with mobile communications (pagers and cellular telephones) and mobile computing (laptop and handheld computers). It's easy to find informative articles in your local paper, magazines, and on Internet Web sites. It's critical to know how the new technology will affect your work area and industry. Stay ahead of the curve.

**Be your best.** Do your personal best every day. Establish your competency immediately so that others come to you when they want a job to be done well. Know your responsibilities inside and out. Keep your skills current.

**Be flexible.** Be willing to learn your organization's structure from the bottom up. That doesn't mean taking a job that you are overqualified for, but if an opportunity arises to learn a new job or skill, then jump at the chance. Adapt to the company's landscape. Each company has its own personality and work climate. Be willing to work late and come in early to get the job done.

**Keep on moving.** Occasionally, you will go through changes (you miss out on a promotion, your director is too demanding, or a project goes awry). Be resilient. Find solutions by seeing it as a challenge, not a problem. When you remember that life is full of challenges, you're never down and out.

**Build relationships.** When you're at work, identify the key players in your office and develop a strong working relationship with them. Establish ties with people outside of your department and your company as well. Those relationships will keep you abreast of what's happening in your company as well as outside opportunities.

## MOVING UP

To become a star performer at your job, consider these power tips.

**Be patient.** There is no such thing as an overnight success. Success is a journey that requires discipline, lots of work, and planning. Do your job well and plot your course. Be willing to alter your goals and reevaluate yourself from time to time.

**Do your research.** Stay abreast of the news in your business. Read the daily newspapers and trade publications to keep up with industry trends and developments. When you read articles that you think might be of interest to your supervisor and others in decision-making positions, pass them along.

**Add value.** Go to your supervisor to find out how you can become a more valuable part of the company. Showing concern for your performance is good, but always be prepared for critical feedback. Consider taking courses to keep your skills sharp. Many companies will share tuition for such classes.

**Request work.** Ask for extra assignments, especially the meaningful and challenging ones that less focused and less ambitious employees shun. This will show that you're interested in doing more than what's expected. It is also an opportunity to broaden your responsibilities and skills.

**Suggest improvements.** Become known as a problem-solver by offering management ways to improve in inefficient areas. It's more proactive to offer to fix a problem than it is to complain about one.

**Update your to-do list.** Continually think of things you can add to your list to become a better and more valued employee. Take training courses, learn new computer skills, attend industry-related conventions, or join in your company's volunteer efforts.

## MOVING ON

There's one thing you can count on in life—change. It's what makes life exciting. This applies to your career as well. There are always new things to learn, experiences to be had, and challenges to be met. Obstacles are opportunities to grow, so if your career isn't working out according to plan, know that life has something better in store for you. Be on the lookout for ways to turn stumbling blocks into stepping stones. Whatever the challenge, you can find a way to use it to your benefit.

There will come a time in your life when you should reevaluate your career. It's a good idea to take personal inventory on an annual basis, and certainly before you begin looking for a new job.

If you've been in the workforce for years and you've been dissatisfied most of that time, maybe it's time for a new path. An experienced sister has a wealth of information and talent that can be shared for the enrichment of others and for her own benefit as well. Identify your skills and create a plan to use them in a better, more fulfilling way.

But first, be truthful with yourself. Is the job you've been doing for the past decade the one you want to keep for the next decade? Get in touch with what you love doing and find greatly fulfilling. You are not the same person today that you were when you entered the job market some time ago.

How about a totally new direction? The idea of a new career may be just what you've been dreaming about but

## FAST-GROWING CAREERS OF THE FUTURE

1. Database manager
2. Computer engineer
3. Systems analyst
4. Personal/home aide
5. Physical therapy assistant
6. Home health aide
7. Medical assistant
8. Desktop publisher
9. Physical therapist
10. Occupational therapist

Source: U.S. Bureau of Labor Statistics

never pursued for any number of reasons. Whatever you decide to do, keep in mind that many, if not most, of your skills will be useful. Mainly what's needed is a positive mind-set. Know that it's never too late to create a new life for yourself. You simply must be willing to do the work of transitioning, making the move from point A to point B. Count your assets. Factor in your education, knowledge, and experience in your field of expertise. Decide if you want to utilize your career skills in a second career or if you want to try something entirely new. The key, once again, is to have a plan and execute it!

# SETTING UP YOUR OWN SHOP

Now's a great time for sisters to think about stepping out on their own and starting their own companies. There are probably as many reasons for starting your own business as there are ideas for businesses themselves. Some sisters simply want to be their own boss, while others seek the potential financial independence or creative freedom such an action generates. If you've got the desire and you're thinking about starting up your own venture, go for it!

First, decide what kind of small business you want. You may already have a clear idea about what you want to do, but if you don't, consider the questions below—they may help you develop a better sense of what you could do. Brainstorming with some supportive sisterfriends is often a good way to get as many ideas out as possible. Fill in the spaces provided and review your responses later.

**Do you have any interests or hobbies that might be moneymakers?**

_____

_____

_____

**What skills have you learned or developed?**

_____

_____

_____

_____

**What do you like to do with your spare time?**

_____

_____

_____

## Finding Your Niche

Let's say you're really good at making your great-grand-mother Carver's homemade organic peanut butter. Why not make a whole bunch, put it in jars, go around selling it, then just lay back and count all the money rolling in? Well, your success will take a little more effort than that, which brings us to our next step: determining a niche for your business. Your niche is the place you want to occupy in an already crowded marketplace. To put it another way, what will make people come to you instead of the competition? Respond to these questions to get a better idea of the niche your business will fill.

**What kind of business are you starting?**

_____

**Is your idea practical? (Does it fill a need?)**

_____

**What is your competition?**

_____

**Can you create a demand for your business?**

_____

You probably won't be able to enter the marketplace with Great-grandmother Carver's homemade organic peanut butter and compete with well-recognized name brands, but you *may* be able to develop a loyal following by finding a place for it at health food stores, organic grocers, and weekend farmer's markets—that's a niche.

## The Business Plan

The centerpiece of any business start-up is a business plan, a detailed breakdown of how you plan to start and run your venture. There are generally four parts to the plan: (1) the description of the business; (2) the marketing plan; (3) the financial plan; and (4) the management plan. Let's look at what goes into each section.

**Describe the business.** This section basically answers the question "What sort of business are you in?" It also describes practical parts, such as:

- A mission statement
- The background/history of the business
- A description of the product/service offered
- How you expect the business to be profitable
- The location and hours of operation for the business

**Create a marketing plan.** A good marketing plan is essential. How will you introduce your business to potential customers? Advertising, of course. But that's just part of it. You've also got to describe:

- Your customers (who are they?)
- The current market (what is the competition?)
- Your advertising/promotional plan (flyers? mailings? giveaways?)
- Your pricing strategy (how much will your product/ service cost?)

**Make a financial plan.** From the beginning, you know that starting and operating your own business is all about dollars

—and *sense*. To know how much money you will need to get your business up (known as start-up capital) and keep it running, you'll need two budgets, one for start-up and one for operating your business once you get going. Here are some elements of each.

- Start-up budget:
    Rent, if you're working outside the home
    Licenses, permits, and the legal/professional fees
      associated with them
    Equipment/supplies
    Wages/income
    Advertising/promotions
- Operating budget:
    Rent
    Insurance
    Equipment/supplies
    Payroll
    Loan payments and taxes

**Plan your management.** In any business venture, the most important resources to have and manage well are people. Doing this takes more than just a desire to "play boss," so spend extra time developing a solid management plan. You'll want to consider the following items when composing your management team.

- The strengths/weaknesses of the proposed management team
- The responsibilities of the management team (define them clearly)
- The salaries, benefits, vacations, and holidays you will offer

After you have a business plan you're proud of, you can begin to think about securing a loan (if you need one) to get your plans off the ground. Banks and other lending institutions often have special assistance opportunities for minorities, women, veterans, and other groups.

Remember, the above ideas are only generalized information about beginning your own business and should in no way be confused with solid business advice from other resources. It's always wise to consult a financial adviser with sharp business acumen, or books and Web sites that deal specifically with your business aspirations. You might also consider contacting your chamber of commerce, business groups, and your local library for more information.

# MAXINE CARR-WIGGINS— IN IT TO WIN IT

After working as a collection agent, Maxine Carr-Wiggins decided she wanted to help people instead of making their lives more difficult. With this mission in mind, the twenty-nine-year-old divorced mother of three began the Houston-based Educational Loan Restructuring Service, which helps students refinance their school loans after they've defaulted. After the highs and lows of six years in business, Carr-Wiggins has helped over six hundred people to pay off their loans—that's over $5 million in loans! Below is some advice she gives women who are beginning their own business ventures.

TAKE YOUR TIME. If possible, Carr-Wiggins suggests giving yourself two years before opening the doors to your business. By pacing yourself, you'll learn a lot about what it takes to be a successful business owner—without the pressure of running the business itself. And with the extra time, you're more likely to screen out mistakes before they even occur.

GET YOUR CREDIT REPORT. Although Carr-Wiggins began her business with a $1,000 start-up loan from her future husband, today she suggests using a loan from a bank to get going—and the only way to do that is by having clean credit. Make sure you obtain your reports from all three credit bureaus (TransUnion, EquiFax, and Experian [formerly TRW]). Also, take care of any liabilities (such as a defaulted student loan, repossessed vehicle, broken lease, or back taxes) you have outstanding before you try to start your business. If you have bad credit, you will continually be taken advantage of.

GET A GOOD ACCOUNTANT. Unless you're a real numbers-cruncher, employ a good accountant to help keep your financial records in order. And don't wait until tax time to call one—for $100 a month, you should be able to find a CPA to maintain your books on a monthly (or at the very least, quarterly) basis.

INVEST IN QUALITY. Whenever possible, go the extra distance to increase the professional appearance of your business. Carr-Wiggins rents an office in an executive suite, which means that she, along with other businesses in the suite, share a receptionist, conference room, fax machine, and copier. Sharing space, equipment, and services is cost-effective, and clients are always impressed by a nicely furnished office (which you most likely can't afford on your own yet). Also, make sure you have a good voice mail system so you catch every call coming in to your business.

HIT THE BOOKS. Be well versed in every element of your operation. Because selling your product or service is the aim of your business, read up on sales, marketing, and customer service techniques. You might even want to take one of the many motivational seminars offered to new business owners. Also, be certain you're computer literate.

BE CREATIVE. Keep an open mind when figuring out how to get the job done. Once Carr-Wiggins traded $450 of her services for $2,500 in photocopied promotional materials by bartering with the manager of a local print shop.

PERSEVERE, PERSEVERE, PERSEVERE. On the hard days, you still have to go to the office—it's the only way to get the job done. By staying committed to your vision, you'll be prepared for success when it arrives.

## YOUR ACTION PLAN

In this chapter we've taken you through the ins and outs of developing the career that's right for you. Now it's time to add all those practical nuts and bolts to your career aspirations to make something larger—an action plan. Just like the mission statement for the soul that you created as part of developing a winning attitude, your career action plan exists to support you and to keep you focused as you move through the working world.

### Your Possibility

Begin your action plan by going back to those lists you created on pages 41 to 43 and refresh yourself about the things that bring you joy and pride. Look at your values and accomplishments again, too. These are the elements you'll use to write a *possibility*.

A possibility is important because it keeps you open to your own infinite potential. After going over the lists you created earlier, you should see a pattern pointing toward your soul's purpose. When it's clear to you, write a brief sentence that speaks to the best parts of you and the gifts you bring to the world. Having trouble coming up with something? Think of the most grand and limitless way to finish a sentence beginning with "I am the possibility of . . . " For example, a sister might say, "I am the possibility of abundant love . . . of utilizing my creative gifts . . . of helping others achieve their dreams."

One way to determine if you are on the right track is to recite your possibility to a trusted friend and have her comment on your facial expression while you do it. Touching on a true possibility will cause your face to light up with excitement and with an energy that is divinely inspired and impossible to confuse with something else.

Write your possibility on the line below.

**I am** _____

## Your Goals

Once your possibility has opened you up to your full potential, you're ready for the next step. You've heard it all before. You need to set specific *goals*—it's impossible to achieve success without them. The reason for this is that concrete goals give shape and structure to your dreams and aspirations (the possibility you wrote down above). These goals should be stated clearly so their meaning is immediately apparent to you, and they also need to be easily measured so that you can get feedback on your progress quickly. To use the example above, a sister with a possibility of helping others achieve their dreams could aim toward the field of education. In this case, her goal might be to become a high school teacher who works with at-risk teens.

Whatever you choose as your main goal, make sure it has a close connection to your possibility. Write your goal below.

**My goal is to** _____

In your action plan, each major goal is supported by smaller, secondary, goals that serve as the stepping stones on your path to success. In addition to providing you with timetables to keep you focused, they will also provide little victories on the way to keep you excited about the new moves you're making.

Let's return to the sister with the goal of working as an educator. To achieve that larger goal, she would need, at the very least, to accomplish several important, though smaller, goals such as finishing college (perhaps majoring in education or some other related course of study). Then, depending on her state and local requirements, she might need a teaching certificate to be qualified to work in a school. A master's degree and/or additional training (for the special needs of at-risk teens) would give her even more resources to use on her career path.

Think about your own goal. What will it take to build to that point? Plan out your path by working backward, and if you need help getting started or with filling in the blanks, find someone already successful in your career and ask her for suggestions.

**Write your smaller goals.**

■ _____

■ _____

- _____
- _____

Remember that once you start down a path, the road may twist and turn and new avenues to explore may appear. Welcome these unexpected developments as opportunities to add skills and experiences to your repertoire.

## Your Future

Just as a possibility opened you up to the wonderful qualities you'll use to develop a great career, placing a future at the end of your action plan keeps you moving forward and your mind and intentions trained on the good things yet to come. Having faith and understanding that success and empowerment are yours to celebrate is exactly the sort of expectant attitude that invites those blessings (and countless others) into your life.

Use the exercise described below as a sort of crystal ball to arrive at a *future* for your action plan. Your future is the vision you have of yourself and the level of your soul's satisfaction with your life. Just as you used the other activities you've been working on, simply envision your life (and specifically your career) as you desire it to be. See yourself as a successful woman living out this action plan to its fullest. Now write out what you see in one or two sentences. Use the present tense to keep yourself focused on the seeds of future success as they send deep roots into the soil of the present. Our sister interested in education may state, "I am content with the shape of my life, and I am thankful for the opportunity to use my gifts for the benefit of others. I am at my most powerful when my efforts magnify the success of others."

How do you see yourself in your future?

**Write your visions.**

■ I am _____

■ I am _____

■ I am _____

■ I am _____

When you review your future statements later, they will trigger memories of all the great work you've done and the accomplishments you've made—something guaranteed to put a smile on your face!

Now let's look at a couple of sisters and their action plans.

# JUANITA'S STORY

Juanita is a thirty-year-old sister from Atlanta, Georgia, living in New York City. She moved to New York to attend graduate school but decided academia wasn't her passion. Now she works for a big entertainment firm as an assistant to the top honcho, but she wants to make a move to something more fulfilling. Juanita developed the following action plan.

# JUANITA'S ACTION PLAN

**My possibility:**

- I am the possibility of self-expression, creativity, and dreams fulfilled!

**My main goal is:**

- To work in and promote the arts on a grassroots level by starting my own business.

**My secondary goals are:**

- Work at a dance company, museum, and/or arts foundation to gain contacts and experience.
- Take business courses to learn about starting my own company.
- Volunteer at a community arts center, teaching drawing, dance, and music to children and adults.

- Spend time researching new trends in the arts to stay abreast of the industry.

**My future:**
- My life is glorious and abundant because I am being who I am, and working hard at something I love: a fulfilling career.

## DENISE'S STORY

Denise, forty-five, recently moved from Boston to northern California after a rocky end to a relationship. She works as a clerk for a successful law firm, but although she makes a decent salary, she wants to get into a growth industry—perhaps the computer programming she studied in college.

## DENISE'S ACTION PLAN

**My possibility:**
- I am the possibility of a great asset—my analytical mind—to build and create.

**My main goal is:**
- To become a computer programmer at a small firm specializing in Web site design.

**My secondary goals are:**
- Take computer programming classes to catch up on new technology.

- Study recent trade magazines for industry trends.
- Attend career fairs at a local college to check out openings in the industry.
- Ask friends in the technology industry for advice.

**My future:**

- Because I live each day using my God-given gifts to establish my success, I am whole, complete, and at peace.

## MY ACTION PLAN

**My possibility:**

- _____
- _____

**My main goal is:**

- _____
- _____

**My secondary goals are:**

- _____
- _____
- _____
- _____

**My future:**

- _____
- _____

The key to career planning at any stage is to make power moves down your chosen road. When you discover your work personality, desires, and goals, and after you research your ideal career or entrepreneurial dreams and set up your action plan, you're ready for the best to come your way. Once you take these beginning steps, all of your hard work and preparation will only help you move through the working world like a real pro. As long as you know where you're going, you'll get there. Go on, girl; it's tougher to sit on the sidelines than to be fabulous. So go for your dream.

Key 4    THE PAYOFF

# Growing Your Money Tree

**M**ore than ever before, we sisters are learning what it means to be financially fit and focused. What's your definition of financial fitness? It doesn't mean a life filled with material things: fancy cars, designer duds, and ridiculously expensive vacations. Trying to keep up with the Joneses has left many a person stuck on a financial treadmill going nowhere fast. It's not about being a "material girl."

Financial wellness is about having options, the freedom to live your life the way you see fit, to realize your dreams without feeling saddled with a ton of worries about your financial future. Ultimately, financial wellness is about financial *serenity*. It bears repeating: Money won't buy you happiness. True wealth is about more than the number of zeros in your bank statement. It's about being financially solvent and experiencing peace, joy, and love.

While life is a spiritual experience, we do live in a material world, and to navigate that world smoothly, your financial life has to be in order. For some of us, the initial goals may be modest: Stopping the paycheck-to-paycheck dance. Reducing debt with a sensible repayment plan that doesn't leave you feeling deprived. Paying yourself by setting aside some cash—no matter how small the amount—on a regular basis. Having little or no debt. For others, the goals may be loftier: investing in your future and planning for a comfortable retirement.

Educate yourself about money and how it works. Take the time to understand how you feel about money and how it affects your life, both positively and negatively. By believing in abundance and developing a prosperity consciousness, you'll know that there *is* enough for you to live a life filled with *real* riches.

To see it through, all you need is a plan.

## FIRST THINGS FIRST

Do you know what you want your life to look like? Where do you want to be next year? The year after? In five years? Ten? To be a truly empowered sister, you've got to have a road map to help you chart your destiny. Rather than having rigid definitions of what you or somebody else thinks you should be doing, your goals should spring from your deepest heart's desire. This is the motivation that helps to keep us on track.

One of the most important things we should do is take some time to do some deep-down soul searching. Go back to the lists you created for developing a mission statement for your soul and a winning attitude (in Key 1); refresh yourself on the things that you value and bring you joy. Use your journal to describe what you want your life to look like, financially speaking. Remember, we're not talking about fancy cars and clothes here; we're moving toward a sense of financial wellness. It's also a good idea to sit down with a few like-minded friends for a brainstorming session so that you can support each other's visions.

Once you're in touch with your loftiest dreams, it's time to ask yourself some hard questions. Which of your financial or money-oriented dreams will translate into realistic goals? Are you willing to do the work and make the necessary sacrifices it will take to accomplish your goals? Which of your goals will take a year to accomplish? Perhaps starting a small business on the side. Five years? Saving for your dream house. Ten? Financing your child's college education.

When you've answered those questions, study each of your goals and write them down on a separate sheet of paper. Each goal should be specific. For example, it's not enough to say you want money, and lots of it (if that is indeed what you want). Instead, write: "I'd like to accumulate $100,000 in my investment portfolio in twenty years." Now break down your goal into baby steps. Your first step might be to attend a financial seminar to learn more about how to invest your seed money. Your second step might be to hire a financial planner. Your third step might be to rework your expenses so that you double or triple the amount you've been saving. You may also join an investment club (see page 195), or (with great caution and good advice) investigate your options through the Internet. Whatever your goal, the key is to keep it simple. By taking small steps, your goal won't overwhelm you. Once you complete one step along the path, you'll develop a sense of accomplishment that will motivate you to continue taking wealth-building steps.

Use the spaces on page 141 to write out one of your financial goals, remembering to make each goal as specific as possible with numbers and timelines. If these suggestions do not apply to you, brainstorm for goals that are right for you.

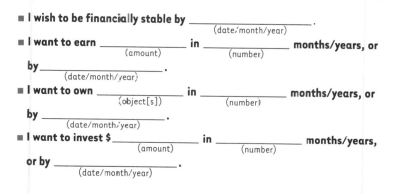

■ **I wish to be financially stable by** _____.
  (date/month/year)

■ **I want to earn** _____ **in** _____ **months/years, or**
          (amount)          (number)

**by** _____ .
   (date/month/year)

■ **I want to own** _____ **in** _____ **months/years, or**
          (object[s])          (number)

**by** _____ .
   (date/month/year)

■ **I want to invest $**_____ **in** _____ **months/years,**
             (amount)          (number)

**or by** _____ .
      (date/month/year)

Now work backward from your goal(s) to get a sense of what it will take to accomplish whatever it is you're shooting for. This may entail taking classes, consulting a financial expert, or visiting a library or bookstore to do some reading up on the subject matter. Use the space below to write down some of your preliminary thoughts, and keep them handy as you read this book. Remember to stay open to new ideas; inspiration comes from unexpected sources.

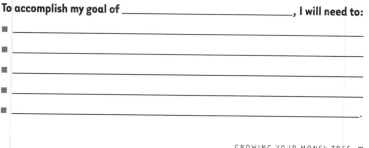

**To accomplish my goal of** _____, **I will need to:**

■ _____

■ _____

■ _____

■ _____

■ _____.

## Your Net Worth

When you've got a clear sense of where you want to be financially, your next step is to figure out exactly where you stand. This means creating a "net worth statement"—a calculation of your debts and your assets so that you have a clear picture of your financial state.

To do this, you need to gather your financial records: bank statements, credit card bills, insurance policies, car notes, pension statements, stocks, bonds, money market accounts, mutual funds, mortgage—the whole shebang. It's crucial that you have the most current records possible. If you're missing records, ask your bank for copies and keep them in a safe place. Check the *Blue Book*—the automobile price guide published by the National Automobile Dealers Association—for the value of your car. Call the benefits representative on your job to find out what your pension and other retirement benefits are worth. It'll take a little sleuthing, but at the end of it all, you'll be familiar with all your assets and liabilities.

Once you've got everything in front of you, make the process as pleasant as possible. Pour yourself a cup of tea and put on your favorite easy music. Then take a piece of

## MY NET WORTH (BALANCE SHEET)

| My Financial Assets | My Financial Liabilities |
|---|---|
| Cash: _____ | Mortgage/rent: _____ |
| Bank accounts: _____ | Credit card payments: _____ |
| Life insurance: _____ | Student loan payments: _____ |
| Home: _____ | Car payments: _____ |
| Other real estate: _____ | Tax payments: _____ |
| Stocks/bonds: _____ | Miscellaneous: _____ |
| TOTAL ASSETS: _____ | TOTAL LIABILITIES: _____ |

TOTAL ASSETS _____ − TOTAL LIABILITIES _____ = _____ (TOTAL NET WORTH)

paper and divide it in half. On one side, list all your financial assets—anything you own that has cash value: cash and checking accounts, the cash value on your life insurance, your home, other real estate, stocks, jewelry, household goods. Tally the numbers and write down the total at the bottom. Next, on the other side of the paper, write down all your liabilities—that is, outstanding debts: any money you owe on everything from your mortgage or your rent, to credit card totals, to student loans, taxes, car note, etc. Add all the numbers in that column. Finally, subtract your liabilities total from your assets total. This figure represents your total net worth.

Ideally, your assets should outweigh your liabilities, but either way, your net worth will increase each year. Once you put your asset-building plan in place and begin to work it, don't be discouraged if your net worth is low or a negative number. It just means that you have some serious work to do. Praise yourself for having the courage to begin. Facing facts is a powerful first step to a fulfilling future.

Your next step will be to calculate your debt ratio. Determining your debt-to-income ratio is a crucial component of growing your money tree because it points directly to the percentage of debt that eats up your take-home pay. Now gather your pay stubs and your outstanding bills, credit card statements, car notes, bank statements from an extended line of credit, monthly IRS statements, etc. On one line, write down your monthly take-home pay. On the next line, write down the total of your present monthly credit obligations. (Do not factor your mortgage or rent into this equation because they're not debt that you have accumulated; they're

Here's how Simone, a young sister who just started her first job, calculates her personal debt ratio.

$1,200    Monthly take-home salary (net pay)
$480    Monthly expenses (not including mortgage or rent)

She divided her monthly expenses by her take-home salary to find out her personal debt ratio.

$$\$480 \div \$1,200 = .4 \text{ or } 40\%$$

This means that 40 percent of her monthly income goes toward paying her bills. A money-savvy sister should try to have a debt ratio of between 20 percent and 30 percent.

ongoing expenses.) Divide your credit obligations (line 2) by your take-home pay (line 1). The result is your personal debt ratio. Most experts believe that figure shouldn't exceed 20 to 30 percent. A caveat: Student loans may push that percentage up quite a bit. And in these credit-crazy times, many creditors will allow for even higher percentages when loaning you even more money, thereby increasing your debt load that much more.

Don't feel frustrated if the numbers look a little scary. Remember, you are taking charge of your financial future. And the future will look rosier every day as you pay attention to and monitor what you do with your money.

## GETTING DOWN TO BASICS: ORGANIZING YOUR FINANCIAL LIFE

Few things create the peace that comes from gaining clarity about your finances and getting your house in order. On a practical level, organized finances will save you time, and even money. You'll know exactly where that business receipt is hiding when tax time rolls around—or in the event of a tax audit. On a spiritual level, clearing your home of clutter sweeps out stagnant energy and makes way for the positive energy you want to welcome into your life.

By calculating your net worth and your debt-to-income ratio, you're already making considerable progress. And if excessive clutter is clogging your home and your mind, get to work. Start a filing system for your bills and important financial papers. All you need are a small file box, a handful of manila files, and some labels. Organize them in alphabetical order and create corresponding files for them: credit cards, utilities, etc. Bills should be kept for up to one year. If you need records for tax purposes, then they should be kept for up to five years. Canceled checks and bank statements should be kept for ten years. Bank statements, income tax returns, insurance policies, investment transactions, property tax records, and copies of your will can all be kept safely at home. Original copies of wills as well as birth, death, and marriage certificates, real estate deeds, car titles, passports, contracts, citizenship papers, military service papers, and adoption papers should be kept in a fireproof box at home, or in a safe-deposit box. And make sure your family or a trusted friend knows what's where in case of any emergency.

## Writing Down Your Numbers

Some of us are money management divas and always know the bottom line in our checking accounts. If that's the case, we salute you. But for many of us, we reach into our wallets, see a lonely ten-spot peeking out, and wonder where the cash went. Thankfully, there is an antidote to the hole-in-the-wallet syndrome: writing down what you spend.

You'll need a small, wallet-size notebook to carry with you at all times. Any time you spend money, even if it's twenty-five cents for the parking meter, write it down: "25 cents, parking meter." It's important to note the amount to the penny. If you take in money that day, whether it's a gift or a paycheck, write that down, too. The key is to keep a clear record of your money and its comings and goings. By writing down your expenditures, where your money goes ceases to be a mystery. You'll know *exactly* where your money went and can easily eliminate wasteful spending habits.

At the end of the week, divide your expenditures into categories: food/groceries, transportation, household duties (such as laundry), and entertainment, as well as any other expenses you incur on a weekly basis.

**Tally your expenses.**
- Food/groceries _____
- Transportation _____
- Household duties (laundry, etc.) _____
- Entertainment _____
- Miscellaneous _____
- Weekly total _____

**At the end of the month, add up your expenses in each category.**

■ Monthly food/groceries _____

■ Monthly transportation _____

■ Monthly household duties (laundry, etc.) _____

■ Monthly entertainment _____

■ Monthly miscellaneous _____

■ Monthly _____

Now you have in hand valuable clues pointing to where you might be spending too much—or too little. Maybe you're overindulging in daily decaf double lattes at the local coffee shop and underindulging in much-needed massages to ease your back pain. Or perhaps you're short-changing yourself in the medical department and spending a little too lavishly on clothes. Writing down your numbers brings clarity and, with it, correction. To move on to the next step, you'll need to have that habit firmly in hand.

## A FRESH STEP: YOUR SPENDING PLAN

Who likes budgets? Just the idea of them implies a Scrooge-like existence of scrimping and denial and more scrimping and denial. As with most weight-loss diets, for most people budgets don't work: They remind many of us of rigid austerity and severe belt-tightening, leaving no room for the little pleasures in life. Many of us start out on budgets, determined to whip our finances into shape with the strictest of discipline. But all too often, when confronted with an all-work-and-no-play budget, our unruly inner kids rebel and all of our noble intentions are kicked to the curb. A *spending plan*, on the other hand, is all about choice: Choosing to take control of your financial destiny. Choosing how you will spend your hard-earned cash.

Writing down your expenditures gave you a clear picture of where your cash flows. Now, with a spending plan, you can factor your goals into the equation. If you want to save up for a new car, you'll need to add that into your spending plan. If financing a debt-free education is important to you, then that will also need to be a line item in your monthly spending plan.

At the beginning of each month, on a piece of paper, list your net income—your take-home pay. List all sources of income, from your regular paycheck to bonuses to child support to social security and pension payments. Add it all up; this will tell you exactly how much money you have to work with that month. Then list all your fixed expenses for the month: rent, car note, utilities, etc. Your nonfixed expenses are the areas where you have some choice: food, clothing, entertainment, trips to the beauty salon, credit card payments, savings. Once you've chosen how much to spend in each category, subtract your expenses, both fixed and nonfixed, from your net income. If you have a surplus, great. You can choose to spread it out over several categories, or you can choose to put it in savings—a great choice!

Don't panic if your expenses exceed your income. This is simply a temporary situation; you have it in your power to effect a change. Give your spending plan a second look: Where can you cut back? Where can you shift expenses? Do you need to earn more income, take on a part-time job, get a roommate? Think of your spending plan as a guide, a flexible tool that will help you achieve your goals.

To make sure your spending plan is working for you rather than against you, sit down at the end of the month and compare what you planned to spend in each category against what you actually spent. Ask yourself if you are pleased with the choices that you made. If not, reevaluate and shift your plan according to your priorities.

# AMANI'S CURRENT AND FUTURE SPENDING PLANS

With the help of financial planner Pat Martin, we have created a spending plan for Amani, a thirty-year-old single sister living in Chicago. Her annual income is $35,000 and her take-home pay is $2,200 per month after taxes.

Amani's current plan shows what she is spending now, and the future plan shows a breakdown of her projected spending after expert advice. The future plan demonstrates how better money management will reduce Amani's debt and increase her savings.

## AMANI'S CURRENT SPENDING PLAN

**MONTHLY NET INCOME (after taxes)**                           **$ 2,200**

| EXPENSES | | | |
|---|---|---|---|
| Rent | $700 | Cellular telephone | 145 |
| Car payment | 160 | Telephone | 100 |
| Gas and oil | 75 | Credit card payments* | 25 |
| Car insurance | 100 | Entertainment/restaurants | 275 |
| Car maintenance | 50 | Life insurance | 0 |
| Utilities | 30 | Hair maintenance | 150 |
| Cable | 60 | Clothing | 155 |
| Food | 150 | Savings/retirement account | 0 |
| | | Cash on hand | 25 |
| **TOTAL** | | | **$ 2,200** |

*Amani is currently making minimum payments.

## AMANI'S FUTURE SPENDING PLAN

The categories where Amani made wiser spending decisions are high-
lighted.

**MONTHLY NET INCOME (after taxes)** $2,200

| EXPENSES | | **Cellular telephone** | **75** |
|---|---|---|---|
| Rent | $ 700 | **Telephone** | **75** |
| Car payment | 160 | **Credit card payments*** | **200** |
| Gas and oil | 75 | **Entertainment/restaurants** | **225** |
| Car insurance | 100 | Life insurance** | 0 |
| Car maintenance | 50 | **Hair maintenance** | **75** |
| Utilities | 30 | **Clothing** | **100** |
| Cable | 60 | **Savings/retirement account** | **75** |
| **Food** | **100** | **Cash on hand** | **100** |

**TOTAL** $ 2,200

*Amani was advised to pay off her account by making larger payments for a short
period of time.

**Life insurance is not recommended at her stage because she has a policy through
work.

# YOUR CURRENT SPENDING PLAN

See how your current spending looks on a monthly basis. Fill out the categories below, adding or deleting categories to fit your personal finances.

| | |
|---|---|
| MONTHLY NET INCOME (after taxes) | $_____ |
| EXPENSES | |
| Rent | _____ |
| Food | _____ |
| Telephone | _____ |
| Utilities | _____ |
| Credit card payments | _____ |
| Entertainment/restaurants | _____ |
| Hair maintenance | _____ |
| Clothing | _____ |
| Car payment | _____ |
| Gas and oil | _____ |
| Car insurance | _____ |
| Savings | _____ |
| Cash on hand | _____ |
| TOTAL | $_____ |

# YOUR FUTURE SPENDING PLAN

Put together a future spending plan that shows how you are working toward decreasing your debt and increasing your savings.

| | |
|---|---|
| MONTHLY NET INCOME (after taxes) | $_____ |
| EXPENSES | |
| Rent | _____ |
| Food | _____ |
| Telephone | _____ |
| Utilities | _____ |
| Credit card payments | _____ |
| Entertainment/restaurants | _____ |
| Hair maintenance | _____ |
| Clothing | _____ |
| Car payment | _____ |
| Gas and oil | _____ |
| Car insurance | _____ |
| Savings | _____ |
| Cash on hand | _____ |
| TOTAL | $_____ |

## CREATING A BILL PAYMENT SYSTEM

It helps to be organized about paying your bills. Take your monthly bill statements and divide them in two, those that have to be paid the first of the month and those that have to be paid on the fifteenth. Put them in files marked accordingly. Every two weeks, sit down and pay the bills that correspond with the time of the month. If it's the first of the month, pay those bills. Two weeks later, sit down and pay all bills dues on the fifteenth. Make a ritual of it. Designate a certain day—maybe it's every other Sunday at 6 P.M.—to handle your business. In time, with consistency, you may find that you actually enjoy taking the time to take care of yourself.

Note: In this electronic era, it's possible to pay most bills, from your student loans to your mortgage and taxes, through an automatic payment program. The money is deducted automatically from your checking account, eliminating undue worry over forgetting to pay a bill. As long as you've got the money in your account, your bills will be paid on time every month. Just remember to deduct the funds from your checkbook so you're always aware of your balance.

Keeping tabs on your checkbook register is the key to

your financial peace of mind. Each and every time you write a check or take cash from the ATM (automatic teller machine), take a minute to write it down in your checkbook register—you know, the little booklet that the bank gives you along with your checks. Never write a check for more than you have in your account, and don't be tempted to put off recording your checks until later when you have more time. Chances are you'll forget, and later you'll wonder why your checks are doing the rubber dance. Bouncing checks can end up costing a fortune in bank fees—sometimes for amounts that exceed the original amount of the check!

When it comes to achieving balance, some prefer doing things the old-fashioned way—on paper. If that's the case, and you haven't balanced your checkbook in a while, then gather together all your bank statements for the last twelve months. Starting with the oldest statement, subtract and add all withdrawals, deposits, checks, and bank fees. If your checking account is an interest-bearing account, make sure to factor that amount into the equation. Write down each check, making sure the bank recorded the amount correctly. Subtract or add the amount from your total balance.

Check everything off once you've made sure that your

## DIGGING OUT OF DEBT

How do you know if your debt is out of control?

- You only pay the minimum on your credit card bills.
- You frequently receive past-due notices from your creditors.
- You can't save because you're scrambling to pay your bills.
- You have maxed-out your credit cards.
- You use credit cards to take care of the basics, like groceries.
- You have difficulty remembering how much you owe and you have trouble preparing and sticking to a spending plan.
- You worry about money constantly.
- You become upset over your financial situation.
- You frequently borrow small amounts of money from your friends.

If the above scenarios sound awfully familiar—and even if things aren't quite so dramatic yet—you need help. Even if you feel that you have it all firmly under control, it still makes good financial sense to tackle your debt.

First, try to identify your subtle beliefs about money. What did your mother teach you about money? Your father? How do you use money when you feel sad, angry, or ashamed? Do you spend money when you're feeling upset, or shop to boost a shaky sense of self-esteem?

Once you've identified the emotional triggers that lead you to debt, you can begin to change your behavior. Knowing exactly what makes you vulnerable to sabotaging your finances is a powerful first step. Keep a journal. Get to the core of what's troubling you. Pay attention to why you're spending. Instead of blindly throwing your plastic on the counter at the department store, stop and ask yourself: Why am I buying these shoes? Do I really need them, or am I just upset because I wrecked the car?

records and the bank's are in agreement. If the numbers don't add up, go back over your math. Check for missing checks, transposed numbers, and missed ATM transactions. If, after your best efforts, you still can't make sense of the numbers, make an in-person appointment with someone at your bank. That will usually help clear up any discrepancies. (There might be a small charge for the service.)

If you've got a computer, you might want to take advantage of the abundance of personal finance software available. They make the task so much easier, save time, and provide excellent records at tax time. With the software, your computer screen is turned into a giant checkbook register. As you input your withdrawals and deposits, it calculates the balance for you. You can also set up a monthly spending plan with the software, do your taxes, pay bills on-line, download account information from your bank, create a debt repayment plan, and calculate how long it will take you to reach your financial goals.

## PAYING THE PIPER

There are different philosophies about how to best reduce your debt load. Some financial advisers recommend that you treat all debt equally: If your credit card constitutes 20 percent of your overall debt, then you should pay 20 percent of the total amount you've allocated for debt repayment. Others suggest that you pay off your smallest debt first, then graduate to larger debts. Still others advise paying off your bill with the largest interest rate first, then moving down the list to the lower interest rates.

Consolidation loans, where the bank pays off your credit card balances so that you just have one bill to pay—to the bank—are rarely advisable. All too often, once the decks are cleared, you end up with even more debt than before. Home equity loans are potentially dangerous for the same reason, and you put your home in jeopardy should you fall behind in your payments. However, if you are facing severe financial challenges, home equity loans can eliminate your debt, leaving you with a loan that has tax-deductible interest payments. Bankruptcy is a last-resort option that will haunt your credit report for a decade.

Whichever method you choose, the key to your success is consistency and a commitment to avoiding incurring further debt at all costs. Make a list of your debts. Cross them off the list as you pay them off. Celebrate your victories, big and small, against debt.

Make sure that your debt repayment plan allows you some wiggle room so you can take care of your needs with ease while you take care of your creditors. It can be done. Act now. Taking small, consistent steps will make a significant change in the long run.

A final note: If you feel that your financial life is way out of control and you fear that you don't have what it takes to get it together by yourself, by all means *run* for help. Many sisters have found help through support groups like Debtors Anonymous and not-for-profit credit counseling agencies. Check the resource list in the back of this book, or look in your yellow pages for listings. Debtors Anonymous is free. Just believe that help is out there and go get it.

## POSITIVE STEPS TO FINANCIAL EMPOWERMENT

There *is* enough. This becomes more and more evident as you develop a special mind-set that opens you up to getting what you want out of life while being perfectly content with where you are right now. It means believing in yourself, and thinking that if you want something and you're willing to go out and get it, then it's yours. It means being willing to receive.

This doesn't have to be a pie-in-the-sky philosophy that doesn't translate into the gritty reality of everyday life. There are specific steps you can take to build your prosperity consciousness. Check it out:

**Be clear, focused, and balanced.** Clarify your goals and what you want.

**Find work that you are passionate about.** Find work that satisfies your inner spirit and connects to your heart and soul.

**Stay focused on your passion.** Even when life throws you a curveball, when you're on the right path, somehow your purpose and your destiny manifest. You'll begin to understand where you are and what you need to do.

**Every day, clear your mind of clutter.** Keep a journal and every day write down what happened and what bothered you. Or, if you have someone you can talk to—a therapist, minister, or trusted friend—talk to her.

**Rid yourself of any fear.** Eliminate limited beliefs you may have about how much money you can make or save. Know that you can become financially empowered if that is what you choose.

**Surround yourself with positive people.** Positives attract.

**Repeat affirmations to yourself:** "I deserve to live in abundance." "I am now handling my finances with ease. Prosperity flows through me." Write them down or say them out loud. When you hit an obstacle, remind yourself, "This, too, shall pass."

Living a truly prosperous life and being self-reliant go hand in hand. You know deep down that you're all you need to get by. Here are some steps you can take to get there.

**Make financial empowerment a priority.** Commit to the idea that managing and understanding your money is vitally important.

**Develop a balanced spending plan.** Knowing where your money is going will keep you on track to financial self-reliance.

**Learn everything you can about managing your money.** The more knowledgeable you are, the easier it becomes. Read the financial publications and click on to financial Web sites on the Internet.

**Join or start an investment club (see page 195).** It's a fun way to learn about money and surround yourself with like-minded friends.

**Stop sabotaging yourself.** Stay away from spending splurges. Avoid shopping malls when your life isn't going well. If credit cards are a problem, cut them up or give them to a trusted friend.

**Set up a money cushion that will give you peace of mind.** Pay yourself first. Don't worry if it's a small amount. Just do it.

## WATCHING YOUR MONEY GROW

Life happens. Sometimes it happens in ways that can adversely affect your wallet. Other times you will find yourself swimming in abundance. If you plan ahead, you'll be able to ride the ebb and flow of your finances without a lot of excessive worry. You just need to know how to use the tools that are at your disposal—life insurance, stocks and bonds, tax-planning strategies, and so on—so that you can sit back and watch your garden grow.

### Insurance

Insurance is protection against the financial havoc wrought by unexpected events—illness, death, accidents, theft, and serious property damage. There is a dizzying array of insurance options out there—life, disability, homeowner's, car, renter's, long-term care, health, credit unemployment protection—and an equally dizzying array of insurance terms to sort through. The concept of insurance is really very simple: Insurance protects your assets.

Whatever type of insurance you buy, the premium is the charge that you pay for your policy.

**Term life insurance** provides coverage for a certain amount of time. The term may be anywhere from one to twenty years. Once the term expires, you can renew the policy for another term. Upon your death, the insurance company pays out a death benefit, a specified amount, to those you designate as your beneficiaries (those who you identify to receive your benefits, usually your children). This is the least expensive type of insurance and provides the maximum protection for the least amount of money.

**Permanent, or "cash value," policy** is another type of insurance. With this type of insurance, the insurance company typically deducts your yearly premium, administrative charges, the cost of death protection, and a margin for profit.

What's left over is credited to a savings account that accumulates as a cash surrender value. In other words, if you cancel your policy, the cash that has accumulated in savings is yours. You can also borrow against this money, paying a specified interest rate. As long as you keep up your premium payments, the policy stays active. Upon your death, the insurance company deducts the remainder for the loan from what it pays your beneficiaries. Whole life insurance and universal life insurance fall under those categories.

**Disability insurance** protects you in the event that you are hurt in an accident and cannot work, or if you become seriously ill. Social Security offers limited disability coverage; if you're eligible, there's usually a six-month wait before you start to receive benefits. Your company probably offers disability insurance as part of its benefits package. This coverage may provide benefits for one year. Another type of coverage provides benefits for an extended amount of time in the event of serious disability. Generally, you are paid a percentage of your earnings for anywhere from five to ten years or until you reach retirement age. If your company does not provide disability insurance, you might want to look into purchasing an individual policy—statistics show that you're much more likely to be disabled in an accident than to die young.

**Homeowner's and renter's insurance** protect the assets in your home. Homeowner's insurance will cover the cost of repairing or rebuilding your home, the contents of your home, as well as the damage you do to other folks and their property. Let's say your three-year-old leaves his truck in the middle of the living room and your best friend trips over it, falling and breaking her arm; your liability insurance will cover her medical bills if you're found to be responsible.

Renter's insurance, on the other hand, protects your possessions if they're destroyed by fire or stolen. Like homeowner's insurance, renter's insurance can provide some liability insurance both inside and outside your home. Whether you own or rent, it's best to keep costs down by keeping your deductible (the fixed amount you pay before your insurance kicks in) as high as possible—if, and only if, you have the savings to make up the difference.

**Auto insurance** protects both your car as well as your liability for any damage you may cause to other people and their property. In most states, auto insurance is no longer a choice—it's the law.

**Health insurance** is one type of insurance you absolutely cannot do without. If your company provides it, by all means take them up on their offer! If you're not working or are self-employed, invest in an individual plan. Yes, they are often pricey. Yes, finding an affordable one takes some doing. But it is possible. Check into group insurance policies that you can join; look into religious organizations or trade associations. Or you can purchase relatively inexpensive short-term insurance. If you're laid off or quit your job and your company employs at least twenty employees and provides them with group insurance, by law, your company must continue to offer for up to eighteen months the same type of insurance you had while you were employed. You will, however, have to pay for this coverage.

Traditional health insurance operates on a fee-for-service basis. With this type of insurance, you can see any doctor you choose. After you meet your deductible, the insurer usually pays 80 percent of your medical expenses. But this type of insurance is typically expensive, and these days employers are eliminating this type of insurance from their benefits packages. In recent years, managed care has become the order of the day. Managed care is typically less expensive, with low copayments (such as $15 per visit to the doctor) and usually no deductibles. But with this type of health insurance, your choice of doctors is usually limited to those the insurer has within its network. There are two types of managed care programs available: health maintenance organizations (HMOs), where you have to get permission from your primary care physicians every time you see a specialist, and preferred provider organizations (PPOs), where you don't need permission to see a specialist.

If you're getting up in years—sixty-five or older—and are eligible for Social Security, then you are also eligible for Medicare. (Those who are under sixty-five and are disabled are also eligible.) Medicare covers 100 percent of your hospital bills and nursing home care. For standard medical costs—doctor's visits, outpatient services, and some medical supplies—it will pay 80 percent. Supplemental health insurance for elders is needed to cover costs not covered by Medicare, such as private nurses, dental visits, and eyeglasses.

# SAVING AND INVESTING

Saving is more important than ever these days. Before you get started with a hard-core investment plan, review your goals. Again, look at what you want to accomplish in the next year versus what you want to accomplish in five to ten years.

Having a prudent reserve, nest egg, or cushion is important in case an emergency arises—or in the event that your car breaks down. Your prudent reserve should be liquid—that is, easily convertible to cash when you need it. You've probably heard that you should save at least three months' worth of living expenses. That way, if you're laid off or lose your job unexpectedly, you can take care of your responsibilities.

But how much can you save when you're already struggling to make ends meet? The rough rule is to save 10 percent each month of your monthly take-home pay. This percentage includes savings for retirement as well as for short-term goals. If at all possible, save more. If you can only save $10 a month, save it anyway. Some savings, no matter how small, is better than none at all. If you have trouble saving on a regular basis, look into automatic savings plans. In many instances the savings can be taken out of your paycheck so you never miss it.

Once you've taken care of your emergency cash fund, then it's time to move on to investing in your future. Getting on the stock bandwagon is in everyone's financial interest. Investing in stock—that is, purchasing shares in growing companies—is the greatest way to build wealth in this country. Stocks (if you make good choices) can offer a higher return on your investment, much more so than the "safer" options of savings accounts, certificates of deposits (CDs), fixed retirement accounts, and cash values from life insurance policies.

A stock's price rises and falls according to supply and demand. Consequently, investing in stocks means being willing to invest in risk. They can be wonderful financial tools if you're willing to ride things out for the long term. Unlike a savings account, stocks do not pay interest. You earn money on them by selling them for a higher price than you paid for them. Some stocks offer dividends or regular cash payments to investors. Usually, more established companies offer this type of stock.

With stocks, you can make individual purchases based on how you think a company will perform. You can trade through a brokerage house, through an investment club, or you can trade on-line over the Internet on your own. Purchasing individual stocks requires that you do your homework by researching a company and by keeping abreast of the fluctuations of the stock market. If you're not willing to invest this kind of time, or you're intimidated by the stock market, look into mutual funds.

Mutual funds, which are very popular these days, are essentially a pool of money into which investors contribute. The fund manager takes the pool of cash and invests it where she sees fit. Some stock mutual funds are organized for long-term growth, others invest for high returns. Many mutual funds can be started with a minimal investment of $50. Look for low-cost or no-load funds.

Not all mutual funds are restricted to stocks. Bond mutual funds invest in bonds, which are generally considered to be a less risky investment than stocks. For the security of bonds, you usually give up the higher rate of return. With bonds, you're loaning a specific amount of money to an institution, usually a company or the government, for a fixed amount of time. In return for your loan, the bond issuer promises to pay interest on your investment. Interest may accumulate monthly, quarterly, or you may receive your interest at the end of the bond's term.

Which is the best investment for you and your needs? Generally, the younger you are, the more you should invest in stocks—some experts advise as much as 75 percent of your investments. Time is on your side, and the ups and downs will work to your benefit. If you're closer to retirement or are particularly risk-averse, bonds will be a safer option.

A money market account is another type of savings vehicle that sometimes requires a higher opening deposit or minimum balance. One advantage of a money market account is that the interest rate is higher than it is with a regular savings account. Another benefit of money market accounts is that you can write checks against the account. Different financial institutions offer different kinds of money market accounts, so shop around for the one that best suits you.

## TAX-PLANNING STRATEGIES

Nobody but nobody likes the tax man—except maybe his mama. The more informed you are about taxes, the less you'll pay in the long run. The more you plan ahead, the more you will reduce your tax liabilities and your tax bill. Did that perk up your ears? Read on for ways to reduce your tax bill.

**Take advantage of earned income deferral.** For the employed or self-employed, you can use salary reduction plans like an Individual Retirement Account (IRA) or a 401(k) plan, a tax-sheltered annuity, or other pension plans to reduce the amount you pay Uncle Sam. Basically, you defer—or postpone—paying taxes on every dollar you invest in these plans until a time when you need those funds—that is, retirement—and will most likely be in a lower tax bracket. Because in many cases you're investing a portion of your taxable income in these plans, your tax liability falls and therefore you end up paying less in taxes. You can take out loans against these plans and there is usually a limit on how much you can contribute each year. Warning: If you withdraw your savings from these plans before you reach retirement age, you can expect to pay a whopping penalty fee in taxes, unless you've done so for medical emergencies, education funding, or first-time home purchases.

**Defer your interest income.** Buy Treasury bills, municipal bonds, savings bonds, life insurance policies, or annuities (a contract with an insurer with payments spread out over a specific number of years).

**Make charitable contributions to organizations that you believe in.** You'll need a receipt or canceled check of the amount you gave the charity come tax time.

**Own your own home.** Mortgage interest and property taxes continue to be fully deductible.

**Sell your home.** If you're over fifty-five and have owned and lived in your home for three of the five years preceding the sale, you may qualify to exclude up to $125,000 of the capital you gain from selling your home. If you're under fifty-five, you can defer taxes on the sale by reinvesting in another home of greater or equal value.

**Shift your income.** If you own your own business, pay your children for work they perform. They'll be taxed at a lower rate than you will be. Or you can place money in your child's name in a custodial account, providing that she is under fourteen years of age. The money legally becomes hers upon her eighteenth birthday.

**Claim tax credits.** Claim 20 to 30 percent for expenses incurred caring for children or spouses who can't care for themselves. In some instances, you can even claim day care and baby-sitting expenses.

**Invest in a tax-free money market.** That way, you can earn tax-free interest on your cash—and withdraw your money any time you choose.

## HOME OWNERSHIP

As previous generations of African Americans learned, investing in real estate is a time-honored tool for increasing your wealth. Indeed, if you're seeking financial freedom, owning your home and other real estate is crucial. To do this, you'll need to learn about the real estate market, as well as get to know bankers, real estate attorneys, and real estate brokers who will help you in your quest.

### Don't Believe the Hype

Don't let naysayers keep you from looking into investing in real estate. Yes, the real estate market, like the stock market, has its ups and downs. No, a limited income need not keep you from buying your first home. No, you don't need a blemish-free credit record. But put your financial house in order before you approach a bank or other lending institution for a mortgage, which is a loan for home buyers. Mortgages are most often granted for a ten- to thirty-year period. There are special programs available for first-time home-buyers, such as obtaining a loan from your state or local housing agency; getting a "Fannie Mae" or "Freddie Mac" loan where you only need to make a 3 to 5 percent down payment; getting a loan through the Federal Housing Administration (FHA); or, if you're a veteran, securing one through the U.S. Department of Veteran Affairs. Some programs will even let you buy a house with no down payment at all. Find out all the details, because these programs often place limits on the purchase price.

But before you rush out to start house hunting, figure out how much house or condo you can comfortably afford. The cost of your home should not exceed two times your annual gross income. Your mortgage payments, long-term debts, and major fixed expenses should not exceed 36 percent of your income; the total amount you pay in mortgage, co-op/condo assessments, homeowner's insurance, and property taxes shouldn't exceed 20 percent of your income.

## Shopping for a Mortgage

Wouldn't it be nice if you could write a check and buy a house in one fell swoop? Well, the vast majority of us can't. To finance our dreams of owning our own homes, we've got to convince a bank to loan us the money. This can be a daunting process.

Once you've figured out how much house you can afford, decide what type of mortgage you want. Fixed-rate mortgages offer a set interest rate that never changes through the life of the mortgage (often thirty years). These are best when interest rates are low. Adjustable-rate mortgages (ARMs), or variable-rate mortgages, have interest rates that fluctuate depending on what happens to interest rates in the economy. If interest rates are down, so is your mortgage payment. Conversely, your mortgage payment will rise when interest rates rise. ARMs offer lower interest rates, which means your starting payments will be lower, so you may be able to qualify for a larger mortgage amount. Each ARM has the benefit of a cap, which is a limit to how much the interest can be increased over the life of the loan, in addition to a cap on each adjustment date. Most ARMs are adjusted once a year.

There are two types of mortgages you should avoid. One is

the graduated payment mortgage, where you don't pay all the interest you owe each month. The interest is added to the unpaid balance of your mortgage, keeping your payments low in the early years of the mortgage but ultimately increasing your overall debt. The other is the balloon mortgage. Here you pay small monthly payments for several years, until you are required to pay off the entire balance in one very large chunk.

Buying a home can be a nightmare of red tape and endless paperwork. But there are steps that you can take to make the process a lot easier.

**Clean up your financial house before you start courting mortgage lenders.** Pull your credit report and clear up any discrepancies in reporting. Make sure you've been paying your bills on time for at least a year. Make sure you have enough cash for a down payment and any closing costs.

**Get "prequalified" for a mortgage.** Contact your local bank or mortgage company. This way, you'll get a sense up front of whether or not you'll qualify for a mortgage—and for how much.

Buying a home is without a doubt one of the more joyous, yet challenging, rites of passage you will experience in your lifetime. When applying for a mortgage, knowing what costs and fees you can expect to pay will help you sail smoothly through the process. Mortgages are offered through banks, government agencies, and mortgage companies.

It takes more than a down payment to make you a homeowner. Here is what you can expect to pay up-front on a $100,000 home with a $5,000 down payment, which is 5 percent of the purchase price. These are estimates of some typical out-of-pocket expenses, but remember that the fees vary from region to region.

## Up-Front Expenses

APPRAISAL: $300. An appraiser, selected by the bank, values the property.

TITLE SEARCH: $300–$400. A search of legal records is conducted to make certain that the property does not have any liens or attachments.

TITLE INSURANCE: $675 (minimum). The insurance guarantees that the title of the house is free of any liens or attachments.

INSPECTION: $200–$500. A licensed inspector examines the house, including, but not limited to, the electrical wiring, plumbing, heating/air-conditioning system, walls, ceilings, floors, windows, basement, roof, chimney, exterior, and foundation, to determine if it is sound. The inspector will report on his findings, including any problems. If there are problems, this is an opportunity for you to renegotiate the asking price, depending on the nature of the concerns.

CREDIT REPORT: $50. The bank reviews your credit history to determine if you pay your bills on time and if you have any liens or other credit problems that would prevent you from qualifying for a mortgage.

ATTORNEY: $400–$650. The bank charges you a fee for its attorney to process your mortgage. You may also decide to use an attorney to represent you at the closing. The fee for your attorney is usually 1 percent of the purchase price.

POINT (amount based on loan). The bank often issues a one-time charge used to adjust the return on a loan based on market conditions. One point is equal to 1 percent of the loan amount.

STATE AND LOCAL MORTGAGE TAX. Check with your state and local government to see if a mortgage tax applies to you.

### Terms to Know When You Are Buying a Home

MORTGAGE is a loan given to a homebuyer by a bank for a ten- to thirty-year period.

MORTGAGE INTEREST RATE is the cost of borrowing the money for your house from the bank.

CLOSING is the final process in which all of the documents related to the purchase of your home are signed and all money is disbursed.

CLOSING COSTS are the up-front expenses you pay associated with completing your real estate transaction. (See list of Up-Front Expenses, on page 181 and above.)

DOWN PAYMENT is a percentage of the purchase price that you pay on the house. The amount can be anything from 5 percent on up, but it is usually between 10 and 20 percent. On a $100,000 home, a 5 percent down payment is $5,000 and a 20 percent down payment is $20,000. The more money you put down, the lower your monthly mortgage payments will be.

ESCROW TAXES is the money held in an escrow account by the bank for payment of your local property and school taxes.

LIEN is a legal claim to a property as security for money owed. A mortgage is a lien. The bank has a claim on the property until you have paid the mortgage in full.

PITI is the principal, interest, taxes, and insurance that are rolled into one monthly mortgage payment.

PMI is the private mortgage insurance banks require when a buyer puts down less than 20 percent of the purchase price. The insurance adds from $15 to $75 to your monthly mortgage payment.

**Consider hiring a mortgage broker.** She can shop around for good deals for you.

**Get "preapproved" for a loan.** With a preapproved mortgage, the lender commits to loaning you the money before you find your home. That way, if you find your dream home, you can act quickly.

# FINANCING AN EDUCATION

Paying for an education these days—your own or your child's—is more than a notion. As financial aid awards continue to shrink, college rates are expected to expand by more than 7 percent annually over the next couple of decades. Which means that tuition at both public and private universities will more than double by the year 2013.

By no means, however, does this mean that higher education is beyond your grasp. Starting to save now is the best way to ensure that an education is in your or your child's future. Even if all you can save is just $50 a month, the sooner you start saving, the better. Compounded interest rates work in your favor over time: $50 invested monthly at an interest rate of 8 percent becomes $17,417 in fifteen years.

If you're saving for your child, you might want to look into a custodial account—that is, an account set up and managed by an adult but listed in the child's name. It's an account that allows for some breathing room in the tax department: The first $600 is tax-free income, the second $600 is taxed at a child's rate of 15 percent, and after that it's taxed at the parent's tax rate. (Though if your child is over fourteen, any amount over $600 is taxed at the child's rate.) Another option is to save for your child's education in your own account, or to set up an irrevocable living trust, where you designate through an attorney how much money will be given to your child and at what time. Education IRAs allow you to target up to $500 each year for saving toward a child's higher education. Contact a good financial planner to help you set up a savings plan that works best for you and your circumstances.

In addition to savings, there are multitudes of scholarships and grants out there, many of them specifically targeted for African Americans and Latinos. If your income falls below $30,000, you may be eligible for a government Pell Grant. These grants range anywhere from $200 to $2,300 a year and are awarded on a basis of need. The Internet can be an invaluable tool in searching for scholarships.

Look into college work-study programs, providing students with on-campus jobs. There are also cooperative education programs, where the student alternates periods of study with periods of work in her chosen field over a five- or six-year period. The military offers qualified students generous scholarships; after graduation, you are required to serve in the military for a set period of time.

Then there are loan options. If you own your own home,

you can take out a home equity loan. Or you can borrow against your 401(k) plan. Also, you can cash in your whole-life insurance policy for its cash value. And finally, there are federally guaranteed loans, such as the Stafford loan, Perkins loan, and Plus loan (a loan for parents of undergraduate children). Some of these loans require you to demonstrate financial need, while others, like the Plus loan, do not.

## RETIREMENT PLANS

It makes sense to start saving for retirement, *now*. Fortunately, there are ways to make the whole process relatively simple—and in many cases, it can ease your tax burden, too. Here's a rundown of what's out there.

■ 401(k)s are retirement savings plans that both large and small companies offer to their employees. A certain amount of pretax income is taken out of your check. You decide how much to take out—usually with a maximum of about 15 percent. Some companies match your savings by as much as fifty cents on the dollar. You can borrow from your account but cannot withdraw your money until you're fifty-nine with-

## LATASHA'S STORY

Latasha knows the meaning of living on a tight budget. As a single mother, Latasha, thirty-seven, is the sole source of support for herself and her two young boys—no mean feat on an annual salary of $30,000. At one point she was unemployed for a year and a half and facing credit card debt of $5,000. Even so, she managed to save $7,000 and recently purchased a house for $89,900 with a monthly mortgage of $800. Says Latasha: "Buying the house increased my self-esteem. My little boys have space to play in the backyard. I'm excited about the future *and* the new century." Here's what she did to realize her dream.

- She attacked her credit card debt by paying the maximum she could afford. If the minimum payment was $40, Latasha paid $60, keeping herself ahead of the deadly interest that can accumulate.
- She cut her housing costs by moving in with her mother for several years. With her living arrangement, Latasha was able to pay off her debt, save for her new house, and buy a car.
- Whenever she got a tax refund, she immediately socked it away in savings.
- She took on odd jobs to make extra money. With one of her tax returns, Latasha bought a home computer. With her computer, she was able to start a side business preparing tax returns, résumés, and greeting cards. The profits from her business went straight into savings.
- She took advantage of a matching grant savings program her company offered. Once she saved $600, her company chipped in $1,800—matching her savings two to one.

At one point, Beatrice was an active participant in the high life: big cars, designer clothes, shopping sprees—the whole shebang. But sometime after she hit fifty, Beatrice, a divorced nurse, realized that it was time to get serious about her retirement. Smart move. Two months shy of her sixty-fifth birthday, Beatrice started having problems with her health. She soon realized that her notions of being out there in the workforce until she hit ninety would never become a reality. Now legally blind at age sixty-nine, Beatrice is living comfortably on her retirement savings. "I'm really glad I took action and took control of my finances before I retired," says Beatrice, who recently bought a new house. "I live alone, and I'm able to take care of myself. Now I don't have to worry my children about anything." Here's what Beatrice did to ensure that her golden years are indeed golden.

- She reined in her spending and sought professional help. Working with the Consumer Credit Counseling Service, a not-for-profit agency, Beatrice was able to work out a comfortable debt repayment plan for her credit cards. CCCS charged her a nominal fee for their services, based on a sliding scale.

- Once she paid off her credit card debt, she hired a financial planner, an African-American woman with whom she felt instantly at ease. With her financial planner's help, Beatrice was able to start socking away money in a 401(k) plan and a couple of IRAs.

- She moonlighted, working part-time jobs as a nurse to increase her

earning power. At first, that extra income went to cut her debt load.
Later, it went straight into savings.

- When she inherited a modest amount of money, she used it to pay
bills, reducing her expenses to just the basics—roughly $300 a month.
- She lives simply but well. These days, even with a new mortgage,
Beatrice knows she'll be fine. She can rest easy, knowing there is
enough.

out having to pay a very stiff penalty, although there are
exceptions. Of course, when you're retirement age and withdraw the money, you will pay taxes, but generally at a much
lower rate. In the meantime, as interest compounds, you can
watch your retirement garden grow—tax-free. And because
your money is taken out before taxes while you're saving,
your total income is decreased, giving you a little tax relief in
the present as well.

■ 403(b) plans work in a similar fashion to 401(k)s but are
set up for employees of not-for-profit institutions such as
schools and religious or charitable organizations.

■ Individual Retirement Accounts—IRAs or Roth IRAs—
are good options for some sisters, and whether your
company has a retirement plan or not, anyone can take

Tracy, a thirty-one-year-old lawyer, learned the hard way that running from money drama just begets more money drama. Even as a law student, she knew she was in trouble, racking up over $16,000 in consumer debt—and that doesn't even begin to factor in the tens of thousands she faced in student loans. Still, even though she spent up a storm, Tracy was always able to keep one step ahead of the debt game. She had great credit. A great salary. And she had great debt. She worked at a job she hated because she felt trapped by her bills. One day, when she impulsively quit her job as an associate lawyer at a corporate law firm, Tracy's carefully constructed house of credit cards came tumbling down. Unemployed and feeling panicky, she moved in with her family and hid out from her creditors for months. When she emerged for air and found another job, Tracy discovered that by hiding from her problems, she'd just made things much, much worse. Here's what she did to make herself solvent.

- She faced her fear. The thought of contacting her creditors after avoiding them for several months terrified Tracy, so she enlisted the support of a sympathetic relative for moral support. She called her cousin before she made an unpleasant call to a creditor. And when she was done with the telephone call, she called her cousin back. The support gave her the courage to face often-angry bill collectors.

- She negotiated with her creditors to make reasonable debt payments. Some creditors wanted her to pay off her balance in full, immediately. In most instances, that was impossible. So Tracy held her ground. Often, creditors agreed to accept smaller, more frequent payments over one large monthly payment.

- She committed to not incurring any more debt. Once she'd plugged the hole on her debt, she was able to make real inroads, paying down what she owed.
- She boosted her self-esteem by tracking down every single creditor, even if it was for a debt of under $100—and she paid those debts. Today she is free of consumer debt and was even able to take a huge pay cut for a job that she loves. Tracy says the trade-off is well worth it: "I'm happier than I've ever been. For the first time ever, I enjoy going to work. And I'm not running from the bill collectors anymore. If you can learn anything from my mistakes, it's: Don't run, no matter how bleak things may seem. Call for help immediately."

advantage of them. The maximum amount you can contribute in one year is $2,000. Under some circumstances, you can deduct your IRA payments from your taxes.

Saving for retirement is serious business. Because of that, you may want to seek the advice of a financial planner (see page 192). Just know that in order to watch your garden grow, you've got to take action. It's one of the most empowering things you can do for yourself in the new millennium.

# FINDING A FINANCIAL PLANNER

Organizing your financial life can seem like a daunting process. But how do you know when it's a do-it-yourself affair or time to call in the experts?

Well, for starters, you probably need to hire a financial planner when you realize that you're making money but not managing it well. Your ends don't meet, or you're paying too much in taxes. You're finding it harder and harder to accomplish your goals. You look at the numbers in your investment portfolio and they don't make any sense to you. Or you're simply too busy to take the time to do it yourself.

If you decide that you need help, proceed cautiously. Not just anyone should be entrusted with handling your hard-earned cash. Do your homework before you sign on the dotted line. And take a few steps to make the choice easier.

**Decide whether you want to hire a financial planner or a stockbroker.** A stockbroker buys and sells securities (i.e., stocks and bonds) and provides financial advice. A certified financial planner is equipped to handle retirement, estate, tax, investment, and business planning.

**To find a qualified financial planner, ask a friend for a referral.** Or check with the Institute of Certified Financial Planners (*http://www.ICFP.org*) for a listing of experts in your area.

**Interview your financial planner the way you would a new doctor.** Ask her how long she's been in the business. What are her areas of expertise? Investments? Retirement? Saving for college? See if her strengths match your needs. If, for example, your primary objective is to save for retirement, ask her what percentage of her clientele has similar concerns. Above all, you should feel comfortable with your planner. You should be able to trust that she has your best interests at heart.

**Ask about her charges before you get with her program.** A fee-only adviser will give you a written analysis of investment recommendations. Her fees will range anywhere from $250 to $1,000 for her comprehensive financial plan. It's up to you to implement her advice by going to a brokerage firm to make your investments. A fee-plus-commission adviser will provide you with the same written analysis for a fee but can also implement her recommendations—a good option if you're pressed for time. In turn, she receives a commission for any financial products you sign up for. A commission-only adviser or stockbroker will give you advice but doesn't get paid unless you act on her advice.

Do realize that spending several hundred dollars for a financial planner is a good investment in your financial well-being.

## INVESTMENT CLUBS

These days, investment clubs are hot. Joining an investment club doesn't mean you have to have oodles of cash at your disposal; the average investment club has ten to twelve members who each invest about $50 a month in the stock market.

It's hard to beat an investment club's benefits: They're a fun and relatively easy way to learn about the ins and outs of the stock market. You get to meet like-minded souls who are serious about securing their financial futures. And with others sharing the risk, investing in the market won't seem so scary.

Starting an investment club can be as simple as grabbing some of your friends and deciding to meet once a month. Once you decide how much to invest each month, you can

## Step 1: Gather a Group of Friends

You want to identify women with common goals and similar investment philosophies because this can be a lifelong association. Whether it's a short-term or long-term strategy, make sure everyone is on the same page. Keep in mind, though, that clubs with long-term, slow-growth strategies tend to be most successful. A club should be big enough for members to divide the work yet small enough to give everyone a sense of direct involvement and personal interest. Fifteen is a good number.

## Step 2: Setting Up Your Club

At your first meeting decide on a club name. You will need to vote on officers and determine how much money each member will be required to invest monthly. Average amounts are between $10 and $50, although some clubs have members who will invest as much as $150 or more per month. You should also determine a nonrefundable fee each member will contribute that will be used to cover start-up expenses, including a business license, mailbox, photocopying, and any other costs. Finally, you will need a tax ID number and to set up a business checking account with a local bank.

## Step 3: Research, Research, Research

Initially, you should probably pick companies you already know. Obtain a stock checklist, which helps analyze a stock's potential for profit. It's probably a good idea to subscribe to financial publications, stay updated on-line at business news Web sites, or visit the local library for books and periodicals about the stock market.

### Step 4: Handling the Cash

Shop around for the best investment option for your club. You might want to retain a broker, invest on-line yourself, or follow the advice of an experienced investor. (Most brokers charge fees per transaction.)

set up an account with a stockbroker. Investment decisions are decided by a majority vote. Let's say your group decides that it wants to invest in start-up Internet companies. Several members will research the industry in general by reading magazine articles and money magazines, for example. Other members will research specific companies and report back to the group on whether the company is a worthy investment. Once the group decides to invest in the company, designated members make the purchase through the stockbroker.

When joining a group that's already established, make sure that your goals, and your tolerance for risk, match those of the club.

You have a wealth of information to grow your money tree. Now put your plan together and get ready for the payoff.

# Supporting Other Sisters and Brothers

# S

isterhood. There is nothing like having great sister-friends. They remind us of all the brilliant things we've said, adventures we've taken, and how inspirational we are to them. They scream the loudest when we get that promotion. They are the ones who think to call just when we need to hear a friendly voice or with an answer to a problem we have been struggling with for days. With sisterfriends we can share our dreams and fears.

This feminine energy in concert can change the world. Sororities, one of the first organizations that paid tribute to sister power, exemplified the empowerment and bonds possible between Black women. As one of the few support systems for women on campuses, they encouraged Black women to study beyond the two-year schools and aspire for four-year colleges and a wider choice of professions. They also made tremendous efforts in neighboring communities.

And there were quilting circles throughout the segregated south and north where women would come together to produce creative work and to rejoice in each other's presence. In some African societies, women would awaken in the wee hours of the morning and begin preparing the day's meals. Inside the separate kitchen houses, women would pound the meal, share their daily concerns, and make plans for tending to matters in their villages. In all these instances, the powerful associations among women were affirmed and fortified.

When you decide to turn your sister circles into groups whose individual efforts will make a difference in the world, you'll be amazed at the amount of power they generate and find that choosing to make a difference in someone else's life often makes the biggest difference in your own.

## GETTING STARTED

There are so many ways to be active in the community! What do you need to do to get started? Well, the best way to get involved in an area of community service is to choose something that matches your interests. It sounds simple, but by doing so, you'll be more inclined to start (and finish) an endeavor you're enthusiastic about. (Of course, you don't have to choose just one, but it helps to focus.) Here are some of the areas you might be interested in:

## Education

Do you enjoy being around young people? Do you have any teaching experience? Would you like to support children in the public school system? If so, you might want to think about *mentoring*.

## Religion/Spirituality

Is much of your life centered around a house of worship or following God's lead? Do you read many books on spiritual matters? If so, consider beginning or being part of a *prayer circle*.

## Culture

Do you enjoy learning about and experiencing other people's lives? Do you enjoy discussing the diversity of the world? Are you a "film buff"? If so, why not consider joining a *film society*?

## History/Travel

Are you particularly interested in Black history? Are you a trivia nut? Are you adventurous, always down for a road trip? If so, a *travel club* might be right for you.

## Politics

Do you want to make a difference in your community by holding elected officials accountable? Does the electoral or democratic process fascinate you? Do you listen to or watch much political commentary? If so, think about joining a *political organization.*

## Sports

Do you have skills on the field or court that you'd like to share with others? Are you involved in a nonmainstream sport in which you'd like to get others interested? Do you enjoy watching athletic competitions with your friends? If so, a *community sports program* might be right for you.

The answers to these questions should point you in the right direction, but if you've spent a long time doing one thing, don't be afraid to branch out and try another. For instance, if you have been a math teacher for ten years, that doesn't mean you have to concentrate your efforts in that area. Maybe you're also a staunch environmentalist; you can use your spare time to raise the awareness of others. Do not pigeonhole yourself in one specific area. We are all complex beings with many interests and abilities. Remember to work from your heart no matter what. If you have strong passions, follow them!

## ACTIVISM 101: VOLUNTEERING

Volunteering is any sort of work you do or service you render without expecting a financial payoff. We've always known that personal success and the well-being of our community go hand in hand. This happens in many ways and for many reasons. Volunteering with a sisterfriend helps you both grow bigger in spirit and delivers a powerful punch of joy into your lives by soothing the soul. It also provides the opportunity to learn new skills and expand your horizons. When you lend a helping hand, you make someone else's load a little lighter and easier to bear. Many times acts like this inspire others to "do good," and one of those acts of charity might just come back to help you when *you* need it. Being active, on any level, also provides a positive example for our younger sisters and brothers to follow. For these reasons alone, we can never underestimate the power of volunteering in the community. You never know the full extent of the good you do, who and how far it reaches, and just how many people it will help.

One small note: The spirit of giving feels best when it is offered without the expectation of recognition. It feels good to be applauded after a job well done, but always remember your original reasons for getting involved and remain grateful for your ability to help.

## LEND YOUR MIND: MENTORING

Similar in spirit to volunteering, mentoring involves teaching a special skill or talent you have to other people. Studies have shown that young people with mentors or those who are involved in after-school programs are less likely to use illegal drugs, consume alcohol, or participate in violent activities. Instead, they have higher self-confidence, more developed personal skills, and the courage and wherewithal to achieve their goals. Many times this can happen by spending time with young people in after-school sports, arts and crafts, and tutoring programs; your local schools, recreation centers, churches, and parks department will always have a year-round need for your time, effort, and seasoned perspective. In our busy society, many children simply need an extra pair of ears to listen to them as they practice reading aloud, an extra pair of eyes to look over their homework, or an extra pair of hands to show them how to shoot a free throw. Making yourself available to teach, encourage, or otherwise help the younger generation gives you a direct link to shaping the future.

Imagine being an adult and unable to understand the information in this book. That's the case for a large number of grown folks who have gone through life unable to read well, or even at all. Mentoring in an adult literacy program is a great way to touch people and watch their lives open up to much more than they imagined.

If you're a creative self-starter with good organizational skills, why not start your own community mentoring program? Here are some step-by-step ideas on how to get the job done.

**Develop a theme.** Sit down with the girls or boys or both in your neighborhood or in your church or in a nearby school, along with their parents, and begin a dialogue. Ask young folks what they feel is missing from programs in their area. Kids have fantastic ideas and they know what they need. If you give them the platform to talk, you might be surprised at the enthusiasm and the wealth of ideas that come rolling back your way.

**Structure the program.** After you have determined the theme of your program, make a list of the ingredients you will need to put it together. Say you decide to start a college prep program for the young women in the neighborhood. If you want to take the girls on a college tour over their spring break, will you be able to get parental permission? Where will the girls sleep? Will you meet with counselors while you're there? Think carefully about all the details that are necessary to make a program run smoothly. And let your program run its natural course. Programs can be just as effective over a short period of time as they can be over a long one.

**Believe strongly in what you do, and attract others who feel the same way.** It's tough to do most projects alone. Identify people and groups with whom you can work. Maybe a church without a youth ministry would lend its name, or a school that wants to add another component to its extracurricular activities. Contact friends and put the word out about what you're doing. Don't be shy about lining up people to get this program off the ground.

**Develop a budget and raise money.** Are there any start-up costs involved in what you're doing? Draw up a detailed budget for a year's worth of programming, even if your program is scheduled for less than a year. Do not be dismayed by funding. Many ideas can be started for very little money. You can get organizations and people to donate much of the space, time, and goods you need. If you do need funding, be open and creative in asking and searching. For instance, if you received newspaper publicity with a picture of your group in action, maybe a bus or train company would donate transportation vouchers for you to use to visit the college. Or maybe a college's Black alumni or student organization can help raise the money needed to bring students to campus and arrange for their housing. Brainstorm with your group members about who they know and draw on them for financial referrals and resources.

## SOUL POWER: PRAYER CIRCLES

What if you want to help hurricane victims, the sick-and-shut-in sister around the corner, or the family whose mother just passed away, but you don't quite know how to go about it? Consider organizing a prayer group or healing circle. Follow the tips below on ways to set up a group.

**Attract like-minded people.** Place notices in church community bulletins, local papers, or any other widely disseminated publications to which you have access and say what you want to do and the kind of members you're looking for. Then pray about it. Know that you will be led or someone will be led to you with similar concerns.

**Make everyone feel welcome.** At that first meeting, share and take turns talking about your beliefs in spirituality and God. Get to know each other. The groups that discuss and share experiences are often the most effective.

**Decide what your prayers will be like.** Will you pray for individuals who are suffering and with whom you have personal contact (say, a neighbor whose house was damaged by a fire)? Or will you pray for large groups of people you may never meet (hungry children in the Mississippi Delta)? Decide on a list of people or groups or efforts to pray over. Then determine the structure of the group. Will you visit people as a group or individually? Will you make calls or send letters and cards? Decide on the frequency and the manner in which you want prayer to heal the lives of others.

**Assign jobs to group members.** Certain people in the group will feel more comfortable doing certain things: One person may want to send cards, another might like making calls, and another doesn't mind hospital visits. Whatever a person's strengths, set up group responsibilities based on them.

**Ask for help.** Sometimes we need help gaining access to the spiritual wisdom within us or understanding how to help people in need. Invite professionals to give your group training on handling a crisis. Call hospitals and ask if they have volunteers who offer training in working with the elderly, disabled, or others in need. Call clinics, colleges, and churches with similar queries for psychologists or counselors who would donate their time. You can also check with AIDS, teen, suicide, and battered women's hotlines for referrals.

# THE REEL WORLD: FILM SOCIETIES

Black women, like a rush of wildfire, raised the profile of book clubs around the country tremendously in just recent years. How about using the same concept for movies? In addition to providing a little intellectual exercise, film societies can serve as informal support groups, weigh-in stations for transplants to new cities, friendship circles—all validating our ideas about life, love, and family, and giving us a safe space to raise confusing and conflicting notions about race and gender and to grow in our understanding of ourselves. In a larger sense, these film clubs are also dictating to movie houses and film companies what we want to see.

We are realizing that we have to support Black independent filmmakers in their efforts to make quality films if we want to see films that reflect us in the way we want to be portrayed. Here's how to get the most from your film or book club.

**Support the film at the box office.** The first weekend box-office draw dictates how a movie will be treated. If there is a movie you plan to see, don't be cavalier about seeing it in a few weeks or on video—see it now. And always be sure to check that your ticket stub matches the movie you paid for—that way you know your hard-earned cash is going to support the movie you want.

**Be vocal as a group with theater owners about what you want to see.** If a theater owner thinks a film will generate money, he might bring the film to your area for a limited time. Independent films especially benefit greatly from this sort of push.

**Mentor a promising filmmaker.** Your club might identify a talented young director and support her with materials, space, and money.

**Sponsor a premiere in your city.** Use a film as an opportunity to raise money for an organization or a special cause. Bring an independent film to a venue in your city and invite people to pay to see it. Sponsor a luncheon or a discussion with the director.

**Invest in filmmakers or start-up Black film companies.** The truth is, it takes good money to make good movies.

# THE LITERARY SOCIETY

Book clubs are all the rage these days, but there's one sister who has been organizing monthly meetings around all things literary for over twenty-five years.

Harlem resident Lana Turner began the Literary Society in 1982 to gather an intimate circle of friends to meet and discuss both fiction and nonfiction works by writers of African descent. Now, what started out small has grown into an umbrella organization under which like-minded individuals can come together. This simple "book club" has gone on to show independent films, produce plays, and stage poetry readings.

Yet even with all this success, Turner suggests that the Society maintains its membership of fifteen to twenty regular attendees because of the more subtle bonuses that come with the monthly meetings. In addition to reading and discussing great books each month, club members come away empowered by each other's experiences and more knowledgeable about themselves. Turner is also proud that the group's high profile brings the power of reading and thought to a larger community.

Starting your own club is as easy as opening a book—your phone book, that is. Call three to five friends who share your bookworm passions and arrange to have them meet at your home or at any other place where you'll be able to relax, open up, and share. At the first meeting, decide the first book you're going to discuss and who will serve as the discussion's moderator, and get a consensus on what day and time is best for everyone (for example, you might decide to meet every second Tuesday at 7 P.M., or every third Sunday at 2 P.M.). Then, at the next meeting, begin by having the moderator open the discussion, whether with a few introductory remarks, a summary of the book, or by jumping right in with questions based on the reading.

If you've got a group of friends who are into the same thing, says Turner, chances are that each person knows two or three others of the same spirit. And when you start bringing these people together on a regular basis, before you know it you'll have something wonderful on your hands!

Good luck with starting your own club. To help you get started, Turner offers these tips.

THE FEWER "RULES" YOU HAVE, THE BETTER. Having a club with a free-flowing structure keeps things fresh, and the more flexible you are, the easier it is for people to come on a regular basis.

IF YOUR MEETINGS ARE HELD IN EACH OTHER'S HOMES, LET THE MODERATOR AND THE HOST BE TWO DIFFERENT PEOPLE. That way the moderator can help the discussion roll on smoothly, and the host can be free to take care of anything that arises (i.e., the doorbell or telephone).

REMEMBER THAT EVERY EXPERIENCE CAN BE A PART OF SOMETHING YOU'RE DOING IN ANOTHER FIELD OF INTEREST. Staying open to everything that comes in your direction is a great way to welcome the possibilities of sisters supporting other sisters (and brothers).

Brainstorm with your sister club members about possible fund-raisers for independent directors and companies. Host short film competitions. Award film school scholarships.

## BEEN AROUND THE WORLD: TRAVELING WITH A PURPOSE

Always wanted to visit exotic locales? Itching to interact with other cultures? Enlist your friends to start a travel club. You can stay close to home and plan a special trip to the countryside or fly far away to the farthest reaches of the world, but try to travel purposefully. Traveling presents an opportunity to expand your awareness of other cultures and ideas, to see the way people in other parts of the world live. Even opening your horizons to historical Black communities within the United States can broaden your world in incalculable ways. So get a few girlfriends together and expand your horizons! Here's how.

**Determine a travel goal.** Whether it's learning our history up close and personal by following the stops along the

Underground Railroad or helping needy children in South Africa by bringing them toys, you will need to establish a clear and concise purpose for your group. You can word your statement like: "We intend to help children around the world," or "We plan to reeducate ourselves about our history as Black people in this country."

**Research travel opportunities**. Have each person in the group research specific places and come up with a theme and a financial plan for a potential visit. Many countries, cities, states, and islands have travel and tourism offices that offer assistance in trip planning. Check the telephone book for numbers. You can also check with the Chamber of Commerce in the cities you'd like to visit, or the Travel Industry of America, which offers resources. In your spare time read travel magazines or publications that review travel destinations of particular interest to people of African ancestry for additional ideas about places to visit.

**Draw up a budget for the trip and begin a savings plan.** After you've decided where you want to go, you must determine how each member will pay for the trip. Have you decided to participate in a group tour? Will it be one that already is offered or will you plan your own? Will each member donate a set amount ($50 or so) each month for the next year to save money, or will each person be responsible for coming up with the entire amount at the end? Present members of your club with a solid plan that will help them stay on track financially.

**Make final preparations.** Once the group has agreed upon a specific place and budget, you can then ask each member to take on the final aspects of planning. If the group has decided to organize its own tour, then someone will need to be in charge of hotel arrangements, someone else in finding the best airfare or coordinating ground transportation or making up an itinerary. Surf the Internet for inexpensive hotels and airfares and car rentals. Subscribe to publications that include tips from seasoned travelers on saving money and how to have a successful trip.

**Spread the word.** After your trip, tell everyone about your experiences, and encourage them to also travel with a purpose.

# GETTING POLITICALLY ACTIVE

In the twenty-first century, sisters are set to make waves on the political front. Building on the achievements of Black women in government over the last fifty years, we're eager to become more involved in the workings of government on the local, state, and federal level. You don't have to be an elected official to make a difference. Getting involved is easy—and important.

One of the simplest ways to effect a change personally is to volunteer your time and energy in the office of an elected official. You'll be rendering a valuable service, and whether you're helping out with special events or just stuffing envelopes, you'll have the opportunity to witness the day-to-day reality of government. If you don't want to align your community service with a political party (as you might when working for a politician), consider spending time at your neighborhood or community association, which is also a great way to have a hand in local current affairs.

Are you itching to become a mover and shaker? Join an organization of politically minded sisters, or start one of your own. It's as easy as getting some of your sisterfriends together and giving the group some structure and focus.

Political organizations can take on many forms and have many functions. They can exist to endorse or support the election campaign of a favorite candidate through volunteer efforts, host neighborhood voter registration drives to increase the political power of their community, or introduce the political process to young people in their area to help them become educated voters. Well-organized communities benefit from all these efforts and others because they can express their concerns to elected officials. Politicians always have time for areas with large voter turnout—it's in their best interest. It's also in our best interest, as people of color *and* as women. Here are more ideas for deepening the political power of your community.

**Host a candidate's forum.** During election time, it's essential, in order to make informed decisions at the polls, to know where each person running for office stands on the issues. You or your group can invite the candidates to share their platform at a meeting held in a community center, local restaurant, or some other large gathering place. Have them each speak for five to ten minutes before opening up the floor for questions from community members.

**Hold elected officials accountable.** Election time isn't the only time your group should have a high profile. When you have a community concern, whether it's high milk prices at the supermarket or children's safety at local playgrounds, let your elected officials know. Your taxes pay their salary, so a large part of their job is to listen to you. With your organization behind you, your voice is even more powerful. Remember, there is strength in numbers.

**Hold a student oratory contest.** Organize a public-speaking contest by having local middle or high school students write an original three- to five-minute speech based on questions such as "What is America to me?" "What will the future look like?" and "What does my community need?" Pool your group's money and present the winners with a small scholarship, or ask a local business to donate gift certificates as prizes. Be sure to invite the local media to give the students, and your organization, maximum exposure.

**Take a political field trip.** Take your show on the road by traveling to your county seat, state capital, or Washington, D.C. Call in advance to set up a tour of the law-making bodies there, and be sure to arrange to see your elected official during her "office hours." In addition to letting you see the inner workings of our political structure, these trips will give your civic group great visibility. And don't forget the camera!

## BE A GOOD SPORT: VOLUNTEERING WITH SPORTS

Turn your love of sports into another way in which you can impact your community.

First you must identify the people you would like to help. Disabled adults? Lower-income children? Girls? Boys? Think carefully about whatever group you'd like to impact and then read the following suggestions on how you might help them.

**If you have a favorite local or national team,** get that team involved in your efforts. Approach their public relations director or general manager about donating tickets for the group you've decided to work with. Arrange for your group to be invited to a practice session and to meet the players one-on-one. Perhaps your favorite team can also be convinced to donate a portion of its proceeds to the organizations you'd like to help that need the financial support.

**If you are trained in a sport or leisure activity,** you may choose to donate your time and coach a team. This way you will be helping those individuals learn a sport they might not otherwise have the chance to learn or that anyone is willing to teach, like soccer, tennis, or chess. Or you can volunteer to teach a dance or yoga class at the local community center.

**If you are involved in a sports team or leisure activity already,** invite the community you'd like to impact to participate in practice sessions with your team members. Girls can learn to play football. Boys can take ballet lessons. Or you can sponsor a game and donate the proceeds from ticket sales to your favorite charity.

**If you are simply an avid sports fan,** invite members of professional teams to come out during the off-season and talk to teenagers about specific topics. If your target community is teenage girls, invite members of the U.S. soccer team to talk about teamwork and believing in self. Or ask women from the WNBA to discuss their dedication and perseverance.

## VOLUNTEERING OPPORTUNITIES

Here's a partial list of where to look for volunteering opportunities.

VOLUNTEER CENTERS. They serve as advocates for volunteerism in communities nationwide and serve more than 100,000 private organizations and public agencies. Check the yellow pages under "social service" or "community organizations" or the white pages under "volunteer" or "volunteering."

LOCAL AND NATIONAL BLACK CHARITIES. As a clearinghouse for matching individuals with volunteer opportunities, they maintain offices in many metropolitan areas.

PUBLIC LIBRARIES. Look for the *Encyclopedia of Associations*, a multivolume directory of associations that are organized by type. Or ask local librarians for regional directories of nonprofit or social service agencies.

MUNICIPAL OFFICES. Visit the mayor's office, town hall, or a community center. Chat with clerks there or attend town/city council meetings for ideas.

LOCAL COURTS. The judicial system (and sometimes the criminal justice system) uses volunteers in counseling and rehabilitation programs for young people charged with and convicted of crimes.

LOCAL SERVICE ORGANIZATIONS. Sororities like Alpha Kappa Alpha, Delta Sigma Theta, and Zeta Phi Beta are all listed in the telephone book.

SCHOOLS. Attend PTA meetings or school board meetings or speak directly to a school counselor, principal, teacher, or coach.

HOSPITALS OR NURSING HOMES. Many have outpatient programs run by nonprofit organizations.

THE INTERNET. Surfing the Web yields numerous sources. Use "volunteer" as a keyword and see where it takes you. Also, www.servenet.org lists volunteer organizations, along with the Corporation for National Service (www.cns.gov) and the Internet Nonprofit Center (www.nonprofits.org).

LOCAL POLITICIANS. Attend local political meetings for insight into issues.

PERFORMING ARTS GROUPS. Ask local theaters if they need help.

MEDIA. Scan newspapers, magazines, and TV and radio programming for stories on groups that interest you.

LOCAL BUSINESSES. Many have community service programs (the public relations department or human resources office will have information).

As a twenty-first-century sister, it's time for you to look within, decide which of your gifts may be of service to others, and share those gifts in any way you can—and make a difference in the lives of your sisters and brothers. That's how empowerment expands; it's passed in bursts of inspiration from one soul to the next. So what are you waiting for? Get out there and make a change!

## Resource Guide

### Key 1   *On Your Mark:* A WINNING ATTITUDE

**Empowerment**

African American Women on Tour, 800-560-2298, www.aawot.com

Iyanla Vanzant's Innervisions Worldwide, 301-608-8750, www.inner visionsworldwide.com

**Books**

*Acts of Faith: Daily Meditations for People of Color* by Iyanla Vanzant, Fireside/Simon & Schuster

*The Artist's Way: A Spiritual Path to Higher Creativity* by Julia Cameron, G. P. Putnam's Sons

*Calm at Work* by Paul Wilson, Plume/Penguin

*Confirmation: The Spiritual Wisdom That Has Shaped Our Lives* edited by Khephra Burns and Susan L. Taylor, Anchor Books

*Creative Visualizations* by Shakti Gawain, Bantam Books

*The ESSENCE   Total Makeover: Body, Beauty, Spirit* edited by Patricia Mignon Hinds, Crown Publishers.

*In the Meantime: Finding Yourself and the Love You Want* by Iyanla Vanzant, Simon & Schuster

*In the Spirit* by Susan L. Taylor, Amistad Press, Inc.

*Lessons in Living* by Susan L. Taylor, Anchor

*Meditation Made Easy* by Lorin Roche, Ph.D., HarperSanFrancisco

*One Day My Soul Just Opened Up* by Iyanla Vanzant, Fireside/Simon & Schuster

*Sacred Pampering Principles: An African American Woman's Guide to Self-Care and Inner Renewal* by Debrena Jackson Gandy, William Morrow & Company

*Sacred Woman: A Guide to Healing the Feminine Body, Mind, and Spirit* by Queen Afua, One World/Ballantine Books

*10 Bad Choices That Ruin Black Women's Lives* by Dr. Grace Cornish, Crown Publishers

*12 Secrets for Manifesting Your Vision, Inspiration and Purpose* by Dr. Richard Bellamy, PHI Publishing


## Key 2  *Get Set:* TIME MANAGEMENT, SELF MANAGEMENT

### Time Management Remedies

The Banyan Tree Life Management System, 212-877-3246, www.the banyantreelms.com

Order by Design, 323-935-5180

### Books

*Do Less, Achieve More: The Hidden Power of Giving In* by Ching-Ning Chu, Regan Books

*Living Without Procrastination: How to Stop Postponing Your Life* by M. Susan Roberts, Ph.D., New Harbinger Publications, Inc.

*Steppin' Out with Attitude* by Anita Bunkley, HarperPerennial

*Success Strategies for African-Americans* by Beatryce Nivens, Putnam Inc.

*Time Management for Dummies* by Jeffrey Mayer, IDG Books Worldwide

*The Working Woman's Guide to Managing Time* by Roberta Roesch, Prentice Hall

## Key 3  *Go for It!:* CAREER PLANNING

### Associations

Association of Black Psychologists, 202-722-0808

Black Women in Publishing, 212-772-5951

Council on Career Development for Minorities, 214-631-3677

Minority Business Enterprise Legal Defense and Education Fund, 202-289-1700

National Association of Black Accountants Inc., 301-474-6222

National Association of Black Journalists, 301-445-7100

National Alliance of Black School Educators, 202-483-1549

National Association of Black Social Workers, 313-862-6700

National Association of Black Women Attorneys, 202-526-5200

National Association of Black Women Entrepreneurs Inc., 313-203-3379

National Association of Minority Contractors, 202-347-8259

National Association of Negro Business and Professional Women's Clubs, Inc., 202-483-4206

National Association of Real Estate Brokers Inc., 202-785-4477

National Association of Women in Education, 202-659-9330

National Black MBA Association, 312-236-2622

National Council of Black Engineers and Scientists, 213-896-9779

National Council of Negro Women, Inc., 202-737-0120

National Minority Business Council, 212-573-2385

## Books

*The American Almanac of Jobs and Salaries* by John W. Wright, Avon Books

*The Best Home Businesses for the 90s* by Paul and Sarah Edwards, J. P. Tarcher

*Black Enterprise Guide to Starting Your Own Business* by Wendy Beech, John Wiley & Sons, Inc.

*Business Capital for Women* by Emily Card and Adam Miller, IDG Publishing Corp.

*Career Book* by Joyce Lain Kennedy and Dr. Darryl Laramore, 3rd edition, VGM Career Horizons

*Collection Techniques for a Small Business* by Gini Grahan Scott and John J. Harrison, Oasis Press

*Dictionary of Occupational Titles*, U.S. Department of Labor

*Guerilla Financing: Alternate Techniques to Finance Any Small Business* by Bruce Blechman and Jay Conrad Levinson, Houghton Mifflin

*How to Find the Work You Love* by Laurence G. Boldt, Penguin-Arkana

*The Occupational Outlook Handbook*, U.S. Department of Labor

*The Portable MBA Entrepreneurship*, 2nd edition, John Wiley & Sons, Inc.

*Power Résumés* by Ron Tepper, 3rd edition, John Wiley & Sons, Inc.

*Race for Success: The Ten Best Opportunities for Blacks in America* by George C. Fraser, Avon Books

*Résumés for Dummies* by Joyce Lain Kennedy, IDG Books Worldwide

*The Smart Woman's Guide to Career Success* by Janet Hauter, Chelsea House Publishers

*Succeeding in Small Business: The 101 Toughest Problems and How to Solve Them* by Jane Applegate, Putnam Inc.

*Tax Savvy for Small Business: Year Round Tax Strategies to Save You Money* by Frederick W. Daily, www.Nolo.com

*Vest-Pocket Entrepreneur: Everything You Need to Start and Run Your Own Business* by David E. Rye, Prentice Hall

*What Color Is Your Parachute? A Practical Manual for Job-Hunters and Career-Changers* by Richard Nelson Bolles, Ten Speed Press

*Work, Sister, Work: How Black Women Can Get Ahead in Today's Business Environment* by Cydney Shields and Leslie C. Shields, Simon & Schuster, Inc.

## Key 4   *The Payoff:* GROWING YOUR MONEY TREE

### Associations

The Coalition of Black Investors, 336-922-6240, www.cobinvest.com

Consumer Credit Counseling Service, 800-278-8811

Debtors Anonymous, 781-453-2743, www.debtorsanonymous.org

Financial Planning Association, 888-806-7526, www.fpanet.org

National Association of Investors Corp., 248-583-6242, www.better investing.org

National Foundation for Consumer Credit, 800-388-2227, www.nfcc.org

### Credit Bureaus

To request your credit report, call one or all of the following bureaus:
Equifax, 800-685-1111
Experian, 800-682-7654
TransUnion, 800-916-8800

### Government Agencies

Fannie Mae, 800-7 FANNIE (800-732-6643), www.fanniemae.com

Freddie Mac, 800-424-5401, www.freddiemac.com

Small Business Administration, 800-827-5722

U.S. Department of Housing and Urban Development (HUD), Federal Housing Administration (FHA), 202-708-1422, www.hud.gov

### Books

*The Black Woman's Guide to Financial Independence: Smart Ways to Take Charge of Your Money, Build Wealth, and Achieve Financial Security* by Cheryl Broussard, Hyde Park Publishing

*Cliff Notes on Mutual Funds* by Juliette Fairley, IDG Books Worldwide

*How to Get Out of Debt, Stay Out of Debt and Live Prosperously* by Jerrold Mundis, Bantam Books

*The Mindful Money Guide: Creating Harmony Between Your Values and Your Finances* by Marshall Glickman, Wellspring/Ballantine Books

*The Money Drunk, Money Sober: 90 Days to Financial Freedom* by Mark Bryan and Julia Cameron, Ballantine Books

*Money Talks: Black Finance Experts Talk to You About Money* by Juliette Fairley, John Wiley & Sons, Inc.

*The Nine Steps to Financial Freedom* by Suze Orman, Crown Publishers

*Smart Money Moves for African Americans* by Kelvin E. Boston, Puntam Inc.

*Talking Dollars and Making Sense: A Wealth Building Guide for African-Americans* by Brooke Stephens, McGraw-Hill

*Think and Grow Rich: A Black Choice* by Dennis Kimbro and Napoleon Hill, Fawcett Columbine

## Key 5 Keeping It Real: *SUPPORTING OTHER SISTERS AND BROTHERS*

### Mentoring
America's Promise, 703-684-4500, www.americaspromise.org
Big Brothers, Big Sisters of America, 215-567-7000, wwww.bbbsa.org
Literacy Volunteers of America, Inc., 315-472-0001, www.literacy
   volunteers.org
National Mentoring Center, 800-547-6339
National Mentoring Partnership, 202-729-4345, www.mentoring.org

### Sororities
Alpha Kappa Alpha Sorority, 773-684-1282
Delta Sigma Theta Sorority, Inc., 202-986-2400
Zeta Phi Beta Sorority, Inc., 202-387-3103

### Books
*The African American Guide to Publishing* by Robert Fleming, One
   World/Ballantine Books
*Circles of Sisterhood: A Book Discussion Group Guide for Women of
   Color* by Pat Neblett, Harlem River Press
*The Go On Girl! Book Club Guide for Reading Groups* by Monique
   Greenwood, Lynda Johnson, and Tracy Mitchell-Brown, Little
   Brown & Company
*The Investment Club Book* by John F. Wasik, Warner Books
*Just Between Girlfriends: African-American Women Celebrate Friend-
   ship* by Chrisena Coleman, Simon & Schuster, Inc.
*Sacred Circles: A Guide to Creating Your Own Women's Spiritu-
   ality Group* by Sally Craig and Robin Dean Carnes, HarperSan-
   Francisco

*Sisterfriends: Empowerment for Women & a Celebration of Sisterhood* by Jewel Diamond Taylor, Quiet Time Publishing

*Starting and Running a Profitable Investment Club: The Official Guide from the National Association of Investment Clubs* by Thomas E. O'Hara and Kenneth S. Janke, Sr., Times Books

*Wisdom Circles: A Guide to Self-Discovery and Community Building in Small Groups* by Charles Garfield, Cindy Spring, and Sedonia Cahill, Hyperion

## Web Sites Worth Checking Out

www.aalbc.com—the African American Literature Book Club features reviews, articles, and publishing information on Black literature

www.afamnet.com—online guide to Black America

www.bet.com—the Black cable networks' online site featuring information on books, careers, health, music, news, and more

www.black-collegian.com—*Black Collegian* magazine online

www.blackenterprise.com—site features business and financial news

www.blackplanet.com—an online Black community geared to young people where they meet new friends, discuss a variety of topics, and get information

www.career.com—virtual job fair

www.careermag.com—employment tips and articles to help women manage their careers

www.careerpathsonline.com—career resource helping youth and students make relevant and informed career plans

www.ebony.com—features *Ebony* and *Jet* magazines online

www.enterweb.com—a search engine portal for small businesses www.essence.com—hosted by Essence Communications, Inc., publisher of the preeminent lifestyle magazine for African Americans

www.hbwm.com—site hosted by the Home-Based Working Moms

www.ivillage.com—an online community for women featuring information on health, business, careers, and more

www.jobsafari.com—employment information

www.minorities-jb.com—jobs and career information

www.monster.com—jobs and employment information

www.netnoir.com—a Web community featuring news and information for and about African Americans

www.oxygen.com—a mix of Web sites and media for women, cofounded by Oprah Winfrey

www.robynma.simplenet.com—site is geared to African-American women and includes information on Black history and culture, computing, and Christianity

www.sba.gov/womeninbusiness—Small Business Administration business information for women and small-business owners on business development and management support for minority business owners

www.smartbiz.com—how-to resources to help you run your business

www.wahm.com—online magazine for work-at-home moms

www.women.com—business and career information

www.womeninc.com—financial information for women

# Acknowledgments

This book would not have been possible without the dedication of the Essence Books team, Jeannine Chuchan, Monique Jellerette deJongh, Tracey Ingram, Knox Robinson, and Linda Tarrant-Reid. Special thanks to Jan DeChabert, Darlene Gilliard-Jones, Pamela Macklin, and LaVon Leak-Wilks. Grateful thanks to Derryale Barnes, Claire McIntosh, Lena Sherrods, Robin Stone, and the entire *ESSENCE* editorial team. Also, many thanks to Denise West and Audrey Adams. Also to Natalee Huey, Diane Weathers, Pat Martin, Cheryl Broussard, and Freddye Smith.

From Crown Publishers, much appreciation to Steve Ross, Ayesha Pande, Lauren Dong, David Tran, and Jennifer Hunt.

As always, tremendous thanks to Ed Lewis, Clarence O. Smith, Susan L. Taylor, Harry Dedyo, Bill Knight, Jim Forsythe, Elaine P. Williams, Barbara Britton, and the entire ESSENCE family for much support and all the intangibles.

# Index

## About the Author

During the past thirty years, ECI has grown into a vital business of diverse media properties and communications systems that includes *ESSENCE*, its flagship magazine launched in 1970.

PATRICIA MIGNON HINDS, writer, editor, and educator, is the director of Essence Books. She is the editor of *The ESSENCE Total Makeover: Body, Beauty, Spirit* and *ESSENCE: 25 Years Celebrating Black Women*, and the author of nine children's books. She lives in New York City.